Teaching Adults

The Issue Face to Face and Adult Education Sole

The Jossey-Bass Higher and Adult Education Series

Teaching Adults

A Practical Guide for New Teachers

Ralph G. Brockett

JB JOSSEY-BASS™

A Wiley Brand

Published by Jossey-Bass
A Wiley Brand
One Montgomery Street, Suite 1200, San Francisco, CA 94104-4594—www.josseybass.com

Limit of Liability/Disclaimer of Warranty: While the publisher and author have used their best efforts in preparing this book, they make no representations or warranties with respect to the accuracy or completeness of the contents of this book and specifically disclaim any implied warranties of merchantability or fitness for a particular purpose. No warranty may be created or extended by sales representatives or written sales materials. The advice and strategies contained herein may not be suitable for your situation. You should consult with a professional where appropriate. Neither the publisher nor author shall be liable for any loss of profit or any other commercial damages, including but not limited to special, incidental, consequential, or other damages. Readers should be aware that Internet Web sites offered as citations and/or sources for further information may have changed or disappeared between the time this was written and when it is read.

Jossey-Bass books and products are available through most bookstores. To contact Jossey-Bass directly call our Customer Care Department within the U.S. at 800-956-7739, outside the U.S. at 317-572-3986, or fax 317-572-4002.

Wiley publishes in a variety of print and electronic formats and by print-on-demand. Some material included with standard print versions of this book may not be included in e-books or in print-on-demand. If this book refers to media such as a CD or DVD that is not included in the version you purchased, you may download this material at http://booksupport.wiley.com. For more information about Wiley products, visit www.wiley.com.

Library of Congress Cataloging-in-Publication Data has been applied for and is on file with the Library of Congress.
ISBN 978-1-118-90341-4 (hbk)
ISBN 978-1-118-90359-9 (ebk)
ISBN 978-1-118-90377-3 (ebk)

Printed in the United States of America

FIRST EDITION

HB *Printing* V10016204_121619

Contents

Preface

Most of us, at some time in our lives, teach adults. It may be in a classroom or training setting. But most likely, it is in an informal way: teaching a friend or relative a craft or skill that we can pass on, in the workplace when we help a colleague learn a new computer application, during a religious education class at the local church or synagogue, teaching first aid techniques to a group of adult volunteers, or organizing a protest around a controversial issue facing the community. The point is that most people who teach adults do not primarily identify themselves as adult educators. For many educators, such as college instructors, adults usually represent a percentage of all learners. However, adult learning can be found in almost any setting in our society; and where adults are learning, there is someone who is teaching these adults or helping to facilitate their learning.

The purpose of this book is to introduce you to the world of teaching adults. For me, the book presents both a challenge and an opportunity. I have spent my professional life writing mainly for the academic world—those people who identify with the profession and practice of adult education. In this book, my goal is to reach out beyond the academy to share ideas with you in a way that can be read quickly and used as a resource that you can revisit from time to time as you face new challenges and questions in teaching adults. For me the goals are to keep jargon to a minimum and to be sure that the book is grounded in ideas developed from theory, research, and practice in adult education, while presenting these ideas without the extensive use of footnotes and references. I have included a brief list of books for further reading at the end of each chapter for those of you seeking more in-depth discussion. By writing this book, it was my hope to be able to share ideas I believe are worth sharing with readers like you who may be new to teaching adults or who are seeking new ways to reach the adult learners with whom you are already working.

The book is comprised of twelve chapters and an epilogue divided into three parts. Part One, which includes the first two chapters, begins with Chapter One, which sets the stage for understanding the exciting world of teaching adults. In Chapter Two, I describe seven qualities or attributes of effective teachers and introduce what I envision as four keys to effective teaching. The six chapters of Part Two focus on each of the four keys described above: knowing the content, knowing the adult learner, knowing about teaching, and knowing yourself. In Part Three, four chapters address topics of particular interest in working effectively with adult learners. These include understanding the learning environment, overcoming resistance to learning, motivation, and dealing with special situations that can arise when teaching adults. Finally, a brief Epilogue brings the discussion to a close by summarizing main themes and offering a call to action as you begin to develop your own identity as a teacher of adults.

I wrote this book with four kinds of readers in mind. First, the book is intended for people who are totally new to teaching but who find themselves responsible for some form of teaching. Included here are professionals who are suddenly told they have to offer a training session on an area of their practice; the non-teacher who agrees to teach an adult Sunday School class; people who train volunteer leaders in 4-H, scouting, Junior Achievement, or some other youth group; or the historian who is called upon to teach a group of adults about how to do genealogy on the Internet. These are people who have special skills but have not previously had an opportunity to help others learn about what they know.

A second audience is made up of people who have responsibility for teaching adults but who don't think of themselves primarily as teachers. These include ministers, social workers, health care providers, and other professionals who identify with a specific profession but who don't *think* of themselves as teachers, even though they know that much of what they do is teaching.

A third audience to whom I have targeted this book is made up of professors or instructors in colleges, universities, community colleges, and preparatory schools. While this group of educators has had a lot of experience with teaching, they often are not prepared to face the challenge of meeting the unique needs of the increasing number of adult and part-time students who enter their classes.

Finally, I would be remiss if I did not include as one of the audiences for this book those graduate students in adult education or related fields who are interested in learning about teaching adults. While you need to think of this book as an introduction or overview, I believe it can be a primer that will help you identify areas that you might like to pursue in greater depth during your graduate studies.

I would like to thank several people who have helped to make this book a reality. First, I thank David Brightman, my friend and former editor at Jossey-Bass. His belief in and support of this project was crucial in bringing it to fruition. It has been a pleasure working with such a wonderful editor. Roger Hiemstra has been a constant source of inspiration to me throughout my entire teaching career. He has been my teacher, mentor, colleague, collaborator, and, most important, a trusted friend. Nearly everything I know about teaching adults has been touched in some way by Roger's example, experience, and writings. I would also like to thank the many students I have taught over more than three decades, first at Syracuse University, then at

Montana State University and, since 1988, at the University of Tennessee. I am especially grateful to several students over the past two or three years whose encouragement to write this book truly convinced me that I needed to do it, as well as several students who read earlier drafts of the book in my "Facilitating Adult Learning" course and gave me valuable feedback. Finally, I want to thank my wife, Mary Rowden Brockett, for her support, encouragement, nudging, and, most important, her love. You have truly been the best part of me.

Teaching adults is a journey ... one that is filled with joy, excitement, fear, frustration, doubt, and possibility. My hope is that this book will, in some small way, serve as a map to guide you on your journey. Happy travels.

Ralph G. Brockett
August 2014

About the Author

Ralph G. Brockett, Ph.D., is a professor and the interim head of the Department of Educational Psychology and Counseling at the University of Tennessee, Knoxville. He received his B.A. in psychology and his M.Ed. in guidance and counseling from the University of Toledo, and his Ph.D. in adult education from Syracuse University. Previously, he held faculty positions at Montana State University (1984–1988) and Syracuse University (1982–1984) and has worked in continuing education for health and human services professionals. He is past chair of the Commission of Professors of Adult Education and has served on the board of the American Association for Adult and Continuing Education. In addition, he is a past editor-in-chief of *New Directions for Adult and Continuing Education* and co-editor of *Adult Learning*, and has served on the editorial boards of four adult education journals. He received the Malcolm Knowles Memorial Self-Directed Learning Award in 2004, was inducted into the International Adult and Continuing Education Hall of Fame in 2005, and was co-recipient of the AAACE Cyril O. Houle Award for Outstanding Literature in Adult Education in 1997 and the Imogene Okes Research Award in 2012.

Among Dr. Brockett's previous books are *The Profession and Practice of Adult Education* (1997; updated 2007, with S.B. Merriam); *Toward Ethical Practice* (2004, with R. Hiemstra); *The Power and Potential of Collaborative Learning Partnerships* (1998, co-edited with I.M. Saltiel and A. Sgroi); *Overcoming*

Resistance to Self-Direction in Adult Learning (1994, co-edited with R. Hiemstra); *Self-Direction in Adult Learning: Perspectives on Theory, Research, and Practice* (1991, with R. Hiemstra); and *Ethical Issues in Adult Education* (1988, edited). His major scholarly interests are in the areas of self-directed learning, ethics in adult education, and the study of the adult education field.

Teaching Adults

Part One

GETTING STARTED

1

SO, YOU'RE TEACHING ADULTS?

Many years ago, a young student was asked by his professor to teach the last two sessions of his introductory psychology class, on classical and operant conditioning. The young instructor-to-be found himself both excited and terrified as he agreed to teach the classes. With only a few days to prepare, he planned to use a combination of lecture, brief discussion, and a film recommended by the professor. The day of the first class arrived, and the young instructor entered the room. With a shaky voice, he introduced himself and said, "Dr. Burns won't be able to be here for the last two classes so I will be filling in." It turned out to be a long session. The film worked fine, but the lecture was presented a little too quickly and the teacher's lack of confidence was apparent. He did his best to answer questions, but there weren't many, and the session ended early.

As you probably guessed, I was that young instructor. This was my first experience teaching in a classroom setting. What I distinctly remember all these years later were two very different emotions: the first was a sense of failure that I had not done a very good job. The second emotion, however, was a tingling inside that said to me "Whew, I'm glad its over, but *I want to try it again*. This was pretty exciting. I want to teach, and *do it better* next time." As it turned out, the next day's class was cancelled due to a snowstorm and I didn't have my second chance . . . until years later.

I have shared this story because many teachers are called upon to teach without having had previous experience. In fact, very few people who teach adults have had some sort of training or preparation in how to do so. There are graduate programs that offer master's and doctoral degrees in adult education or learning (I teach in one), but most people don't know they exist. Indeed, many people who teach adults really don't need an advanced degree. What they *do* need are some basic strategies and tools that can help them to reach the learners they are expected to teach.

Most people who teach adults do so as a *part* of the other responsibilities in their lives. Volunteer literacy tutors, community volunteers, ministers, social workers, health care providers, musicians, and others perform many roles in their jobs, and teaching may only be a small part of their responsibilities. Likewise, most of the people who teach non-credit courses for school districts, community colleges, or university continuing education programs are not full-time teachers, but rather professionals for whom what they are teaching is a hobby or personal interest. Here are a few examples of the kinds of people I am talking about:

- A counselor at a diabetes center works with individuals and groups to help them learn about the disease and how they can better manage their own situations;
- A public official is invited to teach a session on ethics to a group of public administration students at the local university;
- A young stay-at-home mother decides to become a part-time literacy tutor in order to "give back" to others and to have a new challenge outside the home;
- A social worker teaches job skills to a group of unemployed young adults as part of a welfare-to-work program;
- A musician gives private guitar lessons to adults and sometimes teaches a class for the local community college;

- A retired engineer volunteers to teach an adult Bible study class at church;
- A man teaches a one-evening class on "Ghost Towns of Montana" to a group of interested people from the community; and
- An elementary school teacher is asked to prepare an in-service program for other teachers on how to use whiteboards in the classroom.

These are but a few examples of situations in which people without preparation in teaching *adults* are called upon to do just that.

My purpose in writing this book was to share with you some of the tips, techniques, and ideas related to teaching adults that I have accumulated over more than three decades of teaching and studying adult learners and the people who help them learn. I don't expect that reading this book will instantly make you an expert on teaching adults; for most people, this takes years of experience, along with learning from trial and error. But if you read this book and follow some of the ideas that I share, you *will* be a more confident and effective teacher of adults, because you will learn something about adult learners, the teaching/learning process, and, perhaps most important, about yourself as a teacher.

A Teacher by Any Other Name

One of the struggles I had when I first started working on this book was what to call those people who teach adults. The logical choice is *teacher* because this describes what we do. However, in the world of adult education, the word teacher often brings up images of elementary and secondary classrooms. *Instructor* is another common term; it is often used in post-secondary education at colleges and universities, community colleges, and proprietary schools. In the workplace, we often use the term *trainer*. Learning in the workplace frequently involves training in skills or procedures, so this term fits many situations in which adults are involved in learn-ing. Finally, another term that is often used is *facilitator*. Because facilitator refers to a person who **guides** learners rather than **tells** them, the term works for many educators of adults, but it is some-times thought to be a weak descriptor by others, especially those who identify as trainers.

So what to do? I decided that in this book I will use *all* of these terms—teacher, instructor, trainer, facilitator—as well as educator of adults or, simply, educator. I will use these terms interchangeably and, while there are subtle differences, as you read the book, don't let the different descriptors throw you. Feel free to substitute your preferred term. However, I will most often use "teacher" as I share the ideas related to helping adults learn. Despite the reluctance of many adult educators to use a term they often associate with K–12 education, teacher is the clearest way to describe what we are doing . . . we are teaching! A teacher is one who teaches.

A final point before we begin our journey. I am writing this book for readers who teach in many different settings. These include college professors with increasing numbers of adult students in their classes; trainers in business and public service settings; in-service coordinators in schools, health care settings, and other professions; and the many, many people who find themselves teaching adults, sometimes without even realizing it. The challenge in writing this book was for me to make it relevant to such a diverse audience. I have tried to use examples from different settings. Most of my personal examples come from the higher education classroom, where I have done most of my teaching over more than thirty-two years (that's a scary thought as I write this!). But your job as the reader is to transfer these examples to your own practice in order to see the point I am trying to make. If you can read in a proactive way, you should be able to get quite a bit out of the book, even if the examples are spread over a broad landscape of settings.

Teaching adults can be intimidating at first, as I learned in the experience that opened this chapter. But if it weren't intimidating at times, there would be no challenge. Teaching adults can be a source of great joy, excitement, and satisfaction. My hope is that you will have this in mind as you explore the following chapters. By understanding a few tips, strategies, and techniques, your journey on the road to teaching adults should be a rewarding adventure.

THINK ABOUT IT

Take a minute to think of yourself teaching adults. This can be an actual past experience or it can be an image you have of yourself teaching in the future. Reflect on the following questions.

- How do I feel about teaching adults?
- What are my fears?
- What are the strengths I bring to teaching adults?
- What knowledge and skills do I need to develop further in order to be a more effective teacher?

Now, write down a few notes for each of the questions. As you read this book, refer to these notes from time to time. Have your responses changed? How so?

Notes:_____

_____

_____

_____

_____

_____

_____

_____

_____

Further Reading

Apps, J.W. (1991). *Mastering the teaching of adults*. Malabar, FL: Krieger.

Apps, J.W. (1996). *Teaching from the heart*. Malabar, FL: Krieger.

Brookfield, S.D. (2006). *The skillful teacher* (2nd ed.). San Francisco, CA: Jossey-Bass.

Palmer, P.J. (2007). *The courage to teach* (10th ann. ed.). San Francisco, CA: Jossey-Bass.

2

WHAT IS EFFECTIVE TEACHING?

What does a teacher of adults need to know in order to be effective? Many writers have come up with lists of knowledge, skills, and attitudes that can be found in "good" teachers. The cornerstone of this book is a very simple formula: *effective teaching leads to successful learning*!

Effective Teaching → Successful Learning

In order to provide a foundation on which to build the discussion of effective teaching, in this chapter, I emphasize two things: (1) seven essential qualities or attributes of an effective teacher and (2) four keys to effective teaching. Together, these qualities and keys lay the groundwork for helping you to become a more effective teacher.

A Teacher in Seven Words

For many years, I have used an activity in my course on teaching adults where I write "What Is a Teacher?" at the top of a flip chart. Then, I ask students to respond to the question with words or brief phrases, which are then written on the flip chart. When I came to Tennessee in the late 1980s, I used this activity in one of the first classes I taught. Near the end of the activity, a voice in the back of the room said, "gaahhhd." Knowing that some teachers with large egos think of themselves as "God-like," I began writing "G-o-d" and immediately noticed rumblings of "What?" and "Huh?" And then the man at the back of the room said, "No! Not gaahhhd … G-u-i-d-e … gaahhd." The room broke out in laughter and I laughed, too, as my face turned red with embarrassment. That introduction to the nuances of regional dialect has stayed with me all these years.

So, yes, I do believe that the teacher of adults is a guide—as well as a facilitator, instructor, trainer, or any number of words and phrases. But in thinking about this chapter, I came up with seven words that, in my view, describe essential qualities of an ideal teacher. Notice that each word begins with one of the letters in the word "teacher." Here, then, is my "teacher in seven words":

- Trust
- Empathy
- Authenticity
- Confidence
- Humility
- Enthusiasm
- Respect

Let's take a closer look at each of these qualities.

Trust

Trust is essential in building a climate conducive to successful learning. Trust begins with you, the teacher. Trust is vital in creating a "safe" learning environment, where learners feel free to explore ideas and share their views without fear of criticism from the teacher or other learners. The opposite of this is a climate of fear, intimidation, and mistrust, which can result in students not being willing to take risks in order to reach their fullest potential.

What can you do to create trust? First, you can model trust by the example you set. Giving learners the space to try out ideas and to share freely is a part of this. Sometimes it also means that you share your own experiences with the learners so they can make connections to the experiences in their own lives. Second, you can make sure that you are clear about expectations for the learning activity or class. Be up-front about requirements and about what will take place in the class. Avoid surprising students with unexpected assignments that can create anxiety. Third, and perhaps most important, you need to be willing to *trust the process* and the learners. Sometimes it might feel as if things aren't going well, but before you change direction, be sure that the problem is not just a temporary glitch that will resolve itself if you just trust the process. Likewise, it is important that you place trust in the learners and in their ability and desire to succeed. Encourage them to try new things, even if they are unsuccessful the first or second time. This is part of the learning process, and taking this approach should help the learners trust you, just as you have trusted them.

Empathy

Empathy is an important skill in nearly any form of human interaction. It is one of the foundational skills in counseling and psychotherapy, the health professions, and education. In essence, empathy involves connecting with another person and having a special understanding of what she is experiencing, while still retaining a certain degree of detachment. A therapist can show honest concern for and understanding of a client; yet need not "take on" the person's situation as her own. This is the difference between *empathy* and *sympathy*. An effective teacher is one who is able to understand a learner's feelings and to convey this understanding to the learner. It is important, though, to avoid crossing the line and trying to assume responsibility for the learner's feelings. Again, this is where a healthy empathic understanding can turn into an unproductive and unhealthy sympathy.

You can develop empathy by listening carefully to what the learner says. Be sure to clarify that you understand the meaning of what is being said by asking such questions as "I hear you saying that … " and "It sounds to me as if you … ." By asking for clarification in this way, you are communicating that you care about what the learner is saying and that you want to develop a deeper understanding of the feelings being conveyed.

Authenticity

Authenticity is another word for "genuineness," which means being yourself. An authentic teacher is one who does not put on a front or try to be something that she is not. A famous quote from Shakespeare's *Hamlet*, "To thine own self be true" reflects authenticity. At its best, authenticity means to be yourself and to use those elements of who you are to the best of your ability. If it comes naturally for you to be a highly dynamic teacher who is good at teaching by "entertaining," then follow that direction. On the other hand, if you tend to be more reserved or introverted, don't feel that you have to put on airs in order to keep learners entertained. Just be yourself and use what you possess to the best of your ability. We will discuss this in greater detail in Chapter Eight, when we look at the notion of personal style.

Confidence

Effective teachers are confident teachers. They are confident about what they know and how to share it with others. Confidence grows with experience. As you see your learners succeed, your confidence should continue to increase. At its best, confidence means having a sense of self-assuredness that should transfer to the learners, helping them, in turn, to be confident that what they are being taught is relevant, important, and correct. Praising good efforts and correcting incorrect answers in a non-intimidating way can go a long way to building learner confidence.

In a way, however, confidence is a double-edged sword. Too little confidence will mean that learners won't have faith in your teaching. Too much confidence, and you risk coming across as arrogant or as a "know-it-all." This is why the next quality, humility, is especially important. We will look more closely at confidence in Chapter Eleven on motivation.

Humility

An effective teacher is one who is able to demonstrate mastery of a topic without coming across as self-important. According to the Merriam-Webster dictionary, humility is synonymous with *modesty* or *down-to-earthness*. Humble teachers recognize that, although they possess specialized knowledge and skills, along with a special ability to share what they know, they are able to hold their ego in check and not let knowledge and authority go to their heads. In other words, they know their stuff and they let their actions work for them without the need to prove anything or convince others of their importance.

A humble teacher is one who does not always have to be right and is not threatened by students or other teachers who know something that she doesn't know. Humble teachers do not take themselves too seriously and, in fact, are willing to turn humor or a story of failure on themselves to show their own vulnerability. This authentic response can be an effective strategy for building trust among learners.

Enthusiasm

Of the seven qualities discussed here, enthusiasm is one of the most crucial. One can possess each of the other qualities, but without an ability to demonstrate enthusiasm, it will be nearly impossible to reach the learners. Enthusiasm means different things to different people. For some, an enthusiastic teacher is one who is "bubbly" and full of energy; this person treats teaching as a performance. On the other hand, some teachers show their enthusiasm in a more quiet, reserved way. These teachers convey enthusiasm through a love of their topic and an ability to share in a way that clearly demonstrates excitement for what they are teaching.

The essential point is that the enthusiastic teacher gives a clear message that "I love what I am doing and am happy to be here doing what I am doing. I care about getting the learners excited about the topic and care whether they learn successfully." Enthusiasm is contagious, but so is a lack of enthusiasm. The enthusiastic instructor is a motivating educator who demonstrates a genuine caring for the learners and for the subject matter.

Respect

Respect means that we appreciate and value the learners, even though we may not share the same beliefs or ideas. To truly respect a learner means that sometimes it is ok to *agree to disagree*. Respectful teachers do not try to intimidate, humiliate, or use their power in order to persuade, cajole, or threaten learners to change their beliefs.

In all honesty, you are not going to *like* every one of your students. Sometimes, personalities and styles clash and, just as in every other sphere of life, there are those individuals you find contrary, irritating, or otherwise difficult. It is not necessary that you like every student you encounter, or that every student like you. What *is* crucial is that you demonstrate an unconditional positive regard for every person in the sense that you make it clear you appreciate the person as a learner. Sometimes this is not easy, but its crucial if you want to create an environment in which successful learning is most likely to be found.

Connecting the Seven Words

You have probably picked up that these seven words are often connected to one another in important ways. For example, confidence and humility go hand in hand. They provide a "check and balance" between the two qualities that can keep from letting one or the other dominate. Too much confidence can be construed as arrogance, and too much humility can lead learners to believe you are unknowledgeable or ineffective. Finding the balance between confidence and humility is not always easy, but when you find it, you'll know it, and you will be a much better teacher for doing so.

Another connection is between trust and respect. One of the best ways to build a trusting environment for learning is to demonstrate respect for the learners. When learners know that you value what they have to say and that you encourage them to share openly, the classroom or training setting takes on a tone where people are willing to put themselves *out there*. And this is where the really important opportunities for growth happen.

Yet another connection is between empathy and authenticity. Empathy and genuineness, another word for authenticity, are two of the most essential skills needed for interpersonal interaction within any of the helping professions. Being authentic and truly striving to understand the world of your learners go hand in hand and lie at the heart of effective interpersonal connections with your learners.

Finally, enthusiasm is the tie that binds all seven qualities. You can demonstrate each of the other six qualities, but if you do not convey enthusiasm for what you are doing, you are bound to fail. The good news is that if you **do** possess high levels of the other six qualities, enthusiasm should come naturally, and if you are truly enthusiastic about what you are doing, it should come through loud and clear to your learners.

Four Keys to Effective Teaching

Next, I would like to shift attention to what I believe are four essential keys to effective teaching. The question here is: "What do I need to know in order to be an effective teacher of adults?" As I stated at the beginning of this chapter, I believe that effective teaching is key to successful learning. With this in mind, here are four keys to effective teaching:

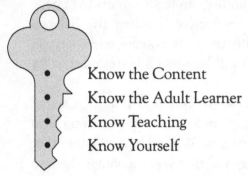

- Know the Content
- Know the Adult Learner
- Know Teaching
- Know Yourself

Quite simply, if you can understand these four keys, you can't miss being an effective teacher. Let's take a look at each of these keys to effective teaching.

Know the Content

First, if you are going to teach adults, you need to have something to teach *about*. In fact, in all likelihood, the reason you are teaching in the first place is because you have expertise on your topic. You have a certain skill or specialized knowledge that you wish to share with others. In some cases, your expertise has developed from years of study and perhaps even college degrees in the subject. This would be true for college professors, including community college instructors. In the majority of adult learning situations, though, you may well have developed your expertise over the years in very informal ways. Think about music teachers, people teaching courses in crafts, cooking, dancing, Bible study, genealogy, or basic computer skills. Still others have developed expertise as a part of their job requirements. Examples here are trainers in business settings who are asked to teach job-related skills and educators who work in continuing professional education or staff development programs. In these cases, the teacher probably has certain related knowledge, but needs to develop expertise related to the specific topic. But the starting point for effective teaching is to have a topic to teach and to have certain expertise in that topic. We will look further at knowing the content in the next chapter.

Know the Adult Learner

The second key to effective teaching is to know your audience—the adult learner. To be sure, certain practices and skills are important in working with learners regardless of age; however, adult learners are, by and large, different from children. In Chapters Four and Five, we will focus on what you will need to know about adult learners.

What separates adults from younger learners is the wealth of experience they bring with them. This can be invaluable for you to help your learners link the topic with their own life experiences. Adult learners are also different from children because, in most cases, they have chosen to be there. Most, although certainly not all, adult learning is voluntary. Thus, adult learners are often eager to learn and are not afraid to ask questions or challenge ideas. This is part of what makes teaching adults so rewarding. But it also means that you will need to be prepared by knowing something about these learners. Chapters Four and Five will help you begin to understand adult learners.

Know About Teaching

The third element is the need to know something about teaching and the teaching-learning process. Often, those who find themselves teaching adults do so without having had any training or preparation on how to teach. At the university level, it is not uncommon for new professors to enter the classroom with strong preparation in their fields of study, but no experience with or knowledge of how to teach. In more informal situations, such as many non-credit classes and training programs, a teacher will have had no experience whatsoever with teaching.

(Of course, this is a big part of the reason why I have written this book!)

A frequent complaint about less effective teachers is that they know the content, but don't know how to get it across. We often hear this on college campuses about certain professors. Teaching ability does not just happen! It takes effort and commitment, along with knowledge and skills that can develop over time.

I was rather fortunate. In my graduate program I took a course on teaching adults and was also invited by my major professor to co-teach a class while I was still a student. Then, in my first semester of teaching, right out of graduate school, I co-taught classes with a more experienced colleague. He was there to guide me through the process, answer my many questions about teaching, and, most important, to model effective teaching. Although I still had a large learning curve, I nonetheless did not have to go through the process alone.

A large portion of this book (Chapters Six and Seven, plus Chapters Nine through Twelve) are focused on the teaching-learning process with adults. We will look at planning and evaluating instruction, teaching techniques, the learning environment, resistance to learning, motivation, and special challenges that can arise in teaching.

Know Yourself

Perhaps the place where effective teaching starts and ends is inside each of us. Jerry Apps, a writer, speaker, and retired professor of adult education at the University of Wisconsin, wrote a book entitled *Teaching from the Heart*, which has resonated with me for many years. In the book, Apps states that "[t]eaching from the heart comes from the depths of the teacher as a person. It is not only what the teacher knows, but *who the person is* [italics in original] that makes a difference" (p. 16). My master's degree is in counseling, and the program emphasized personal reflection and development of skills growing out of this reflection. In fact, many of my seven words for a teacher are skills that I began to develop during my counselor education program. These are, by and large, reflected in what Apps describes as teaching from the heart.

"Who am I?" or, more specifically, "Who am I as a teacher?" are questions that each of us needs to ask. Before we can truly understand our adult learners, we have to be able to look inside and understand ourselves. Chapter Eight focuses specifically on this topic; however, the essence of this dimension of teaching can be found throughout this book, on nearly every page. This last key to effective teaching—know yourself— is often overlooked, but without an understanding of oneself, it is not possible to unlock the door to successful learning for others.

Conclusion

This chapter has laid a cornerstone for the rest of the book. In the first part of the chapter, I identified several qualities I believe are essential in teaching adults. This section focused on the question of "What is an effective teacher?" The second part of the chapter centered on the question: "What is effective teaching?" The difference is subtle, but if you take the questions together and incorporate the ideas from both parts of the chapter into your own teaching, you should be able to overcome many of the challenges that teachers of adults, especially those who are new to teaching, face on a regular basis.

 # THINK ABOUT IT

Come up with your own list of responses to the question "What is a teacher?" Again, these can be words or short phrases. They can conjure up positive as well as negative images. Or they can be humorous. Once you have made your list, look it over and think about each one. What images or emotions do they evoke? My list would have mostly positive images, but if I were to include "Miss Gaetzke"—my sixth grade teacher and the bane of my existence all those years ago—a very different set of emotions surfaces . . . ones that recall feelings of hurt, sadness, failure, and anger. So be willing to look at the whole range of your experiences and emotions with teachers and see what emerges.

Next, look at each of the four keys to effective teaching. Do any of the words on your list fit under one of these keys? Can you think of other ways to describe the four keys to effective teaching?

Finally, how many of the seven words and four keys presented in this chapter surface on your list? Which of the words on your list best describe the ideal teacher? Which ones describe you?

Further Reading

Cranton, P. (Ed). (2006). *Authenticity in teaching*. New Directions for Adult and Continuing Education No. 111. San Francisco, CA: Jossey-Bass.

Egan, G. (2013). *The skilled helper: A problem-management and opportunity-development approach to helping* (10th ed.). Independence, KY: Cengage Learning.

Pratt, D.D., & Associates. (1998). *Five perspectives on teaching in adult and higher education*. Malabar, FL: Krieger.

Part Two

FOUR KEYS TO EFFECTIVE TEACHING

3

SO, WHAT ARE YOU TEACHING ABOUT?

We begin our look at the four keys to effective teaching with "Know the Content." And here, I have a confession. I'm afraid I really don't have all that much to offer. This is where *your* expertise comes into play. If you are reading this book because you are teaching adults or planning to do so, there has to be something you are teaching *about*. Most of the time, this means you have certain expertise on a topic that has led to you being asked or selected to teach. So, in this area, **you** are the expert.

Case closed, right? Well, not exactly.

We can start with the assumption that a teacher has something to teach. But it's not enough to just know the topic. In today's world, where constant change and information overload are the norm, an essential part of knowing content involves *keeping up* with the content. Unfortunately, some teachers seem to live in the past and continue to rely on what they learned when they were students. One of the greatest problems that experienced teachers can face is becoming trapped by the past. Sometimes there is a desire to teach what we learned when we first started. Most experienced teachers, including me, have had to confront this problem at times. But the vast changes in nearly all fields make it imperative to stay abreast of new developments.

Thus, the trick is to know how to balance the "tried and true," which has worked for you for a long time, with "cutting edge" knowledge and skills. In effective teaching, obsolescence is not an option; at the same time, you do not need to abandon all that you know and have experienced in the past.

Two Clichés

I assume in this chapter that you have a certain expertise in your topic. You have developed this over many years of study and experience, and perhaps have even earned degrees or other credentials in your area. But always remember that knowledge is not static; everything changes. Especially in today's world, where it is easy to become caught up in information overload, it is essential to be able to stay ahead of the topic you are teaching.

Here are two clichés that educators sometimes use to describe those who do not heed this advice:

"He tells it like it was."

and

"She doesn't have twenty years of experience; she has one year of experience twenty times over."

I offer these clichés as a way to inject a little humor into our discussion, but unfortunately, all too often they hold true. Now the first cliché may be fine for historians or anthropologists, where their content involves studying the past, but in most cases, we are in fields where the knowledge is changing so rapidly that it takes serious effort to remain current. The second cliché implies that the person does not reflect on her experience and allow that reflection to change her perspective on the topic over time. Critical reflection on experience is one of the most important ways in which we can continue to grow in our expertise.

Teachers as Learners

One way to address the issue of staying abreast of one's area is to remember that, first and foremost, teachers are learners themselves. Keeping up with a topic means continuing to learn about it. You should think of your content area as an active learning project, where you are deliberately and continuously trying to gain new knowledge, skills, and perspectives.

Sometimes, though, you may be asked to teach something that is new or unfamiliar. What do you do in this case? One strategy is to remember that, most often, the best way to learn about a topic is to be asked to teach it. In my third year as a professor, I was asked to develop a graduate course on research design. Now I had taken many research courses over the years and had conducted my own research studies. But the idea of teaching an entire course on research methods was at first daunting. I jumped in and took on my own learning project on research design, reading different textbooks, studying articles with examples of different types of research, reflecting on my own research experience, and developing class notes and slides. The first time I taught the course, it was a little rough around the edges, but I was well-prepared and the students could sense my excitement about a topic that many people find intimidating—or at least challenging. All in all, it went well, and I continued to teach the course for several years, working to improve it each time.

Just a few years ago, I had a similar experience when I was asked to teach a course in basic statistics. Once again, as had happened many years ago, I felt a certain degree of anxiety and even fear at the thought of teaching something I had never taught before. But I also felt the excitement of a new challenge, so I embraced it. As I had done in the past, I jumped in, studied the material that I would be covering, and prepared the course. I'm not going to tell you that I felt like an expert, but I had enough knowledge to share basic concepts of statistics. And I was able to draw upon my years of experience and teaching skills in order to connect with the learners. The course went well for a first-time effort, and I was able to improve it the next time around.

The point here is that keeping up is a challenge you will always have, no matter how long you teach or how much you know about your topic. But if you think of teaching as a form of learning, you should be in a better position to make it a priority to stay on top of your field.

An Ethical Dilemma: When to Say No

In the above examples, I had enough expertise to make connections that allowed me to learn enough about the topics to teach them. But what happens when one is asked to teach something completely outside of the field or area of expertise? This can sometimes happen in the training environment when management needs to have a topic covered in a short turnaround time or in colleges when a department head has a course that needs to be taught and a faculty member who does not know the topic well but needs an extra course in order to teach a full load. This brings up the question of when you should say, "No, I am not qualified to teach the topic." Of course, when there is pressure on you to teach, it can be hard to refuse. But you have to ask whether it is ethical for you to teach something you do not know and do not have a basic foundation to learn. This can be especially difficult for consultants or people who teach non-credit courses for part of their livelihood. You don't want to say no to a chance to make money, especially when saying no this time could close the door to opportunities in the future. I don't have an easy solution to this problem, but I do hope that, by pointing it out, you will be able to reflect and question yourself if the issue ever does arise.

Strategies for Keeping Up

Keeping up is more than a luxury. In today's world it's a necessity in order to remain current and avoid becoming obsolete. There are many ways to keep up with your field. In this section I will briefly share several strategies:

Study groups—For those who like to learn with others, study groups provide an excellent way to share ideas and interact with colleagues. The difficulty with study groups is that it is sometimes hard to find a time when everyone can meet. Don't rule out the possibility of meeting online. We currently have three doctoral students in our program who are separated by several thousand miles, but meet regularly using a current social networking program. Today, distance need not be a deterrent to professional development.

Journal and book clubs—A variation of the study group, the focus here is on identifying books or journal articles that all members read and then discuss together. This approach is sometimes used by teachers or other professional groups in order to keep up with current literature in the field. It is important here that group members be responsible for selecting the readings, rather than having them assigned from the top down.

Professional associations—These organizations play an important role in most fields through professional development opportunities, publications, and advocacy for the field. Trade and labor organizations often provide similar functions. Regardless of your field, I encourage you to affiliate with an organization; it's a great way to join a community of like-minded people.

Conferences—Many organizations host conferences, which are ideal for picking up new ideas and practices and for networking with like-minded folks. Again, technology can provide opportunities for videoconferencing if travel expenses are a barrier.

Social networking—In today's world, social networking sites provide a window into virtually unlimited topics. Wikis, blogs, and podcasts also provide a wealth of information. Here, the challenge is finding what is most helpful to you while not being overwhelmed by the volume of resources available. Start with something familiar and then branch out as you become more comfortable using social networks.

Self-directed learning—As we will discuss in the next two chapters, the vast majority of adult learning efforts are directed by the learners themselves. Just as I used self-directed learning strategies in order to develop my knowledge of research design, you too can devise and implement your own learning plan.

Practice—A final way to keep up with your content area is through practice. Here, practice means two things: (1) it can refer to rehearsing a topic or (2) it can mean going out "into the world" and *doing* what you are teaching about. Consultants or business executives can learn from the experience of their daily practice. Music instructors can seek out opportunities to perform in public settings. Artists can create and exhibit their work. There is perhaps no better way to keep up with your field than *learning by doing*.

In closing, don't forget that you know more about your topic than you may realize at first. Expertise is something you may not always think about; however, it will come to you when you need it. But knowledge isn't static. You need to stay on top of your topic; without keeping up, you run the risk of becoming one of the clichés I mentioned at the beginning of the chapter.

THINK ABOUT IT

Identify several areas in your field where you need to update your knowledge or skills. Then, using some of the strategies presented in this chapter, develop a written plan for how you intend to update in these areas. Be sure to list topic areas, strategies, and target dates for completion. Don't try to cover too many things in a short time; rather, pace yourself over the next year or so. Refer back to your plan from time to time to assess your progress and to modify your plan as new needs arise. Figure 3.1 is an example of a learning contract. I sometimes use this as a planning tool for students in my classes. However, it can also be used to help you organize and focus your personalized learning plan.

Figure 3.1

Learning Contract

Name _____ Course _____ Semester _____

Purpose (Objective)	Process (Resources and Strategies)	Product (Evidence)	Target Date for Completion

Adapted from Knowles (1975) and Hiemstra and Sisco (1990)

Further Reading

Because your content expertise lies in a specific area, I do not have specific
   recommendations to offer. Rather, I encourage you to look at current books
   in your own field, as well as journal articles from your field on how to stay
   on top of new developments.

4

A DOZEN THINGS YOU NEED TO KNOW ABOUT ADULT LEARNING

The second key to effective teaching is to *know the adult learner*. In 1928, E.L. Thorndike and his colleagues published an important study that showed adult learning ability is more stable than previously believed. Since then, educators and psychologists have been pushing back the frontiers of knowledge to the point where, today, we know much about cognitive and psychomotor processes in adulthood and have developed a vast range of theories designed to explain how adults learn. An in-depth discussion of theory and research is beyond the scope of this book. However, I would like to introduce you to some ideas that can help you gain a basic understanding of adult learner characteristics. In this chapter, I share a dozen points and some tips for each that you can use immediately to help you better understand the adults you are teaching.

1. Most Adults Are Actively Involved in Learning and Undertake at Least One Learning Project Every Year.

The number of adults who participate in adult education is quite amazing. Recent U.S. government surveys estimate that about 45 percent of all adults participate in some type of course during a given year. That's nearly half of all adults. And this only counts enrollments in classes, workshops, training programs, and the like. When you include self-directed learning activities, some estimates suggest that nine out of ten adults take on *at least* one learning project a year.

These adults come from nearly every segment of the population. In the past, the stereotype was that the typical adult learner was a white, middle-class, middle-aged person with at least one college degree. This has changed. Today, there is no stereotypical adult learner; participation cuts across gender, age groups, race, and income levels, although the popular belief that "education begets education"—those with previous education are more likely to seek out more education—still holds true. The evidence is clear, then, that there are a lot of people involved in doing what you do … teaching adults!

TIPS: *Remember that, in most cases, the adults you are teaching have chosen to be there. They want to learn. So most of the time, you have the learners on your side from the beginning. It is important to remember that your students will often come from very diverse backgrounds, and you must make a serious effort to get to know the learners. Of course, this is more practical with a small group than in a large lecture class. But even in the large class setting, you can demonstrate respect for all learners and show that you value their diverse backgrounds.*

2. Adults Have the Ability to Learn Successfully Throughout Their Lives.

The old adage that you can't teach an old dog new tricks just does not hold water. Or you could say, "that dog just doesn't hunt" (pun intended!). While it is true that adults experience decline in many functions, such as how quickly they can work, hearing loss, and changes in vision, there are things that you can do to compensate for these losses. Also, while there are declines in certain cognitive skills, older learners typically have the benefit of increased life experience and wisdom, which are resources they can use in lieu of other declines that are a normal part of the aging process. Finally, make sure you create a climate that shows you believe the adult student *can* learn effectively.

TIPS: *Try to adjust the pace of your teaching so that you are not putting older learners at a disadvantage. Make sure you have adequate lighting in the classroom. When possible, use visual aids like hand-outs or PowerPoint slides to accompany your presentations; this will help learners who have difficulty hearing.*

3. Adult Learners Bring a Wealth of Experience to the Teaching-Learning Setting, and This Experience Can Be a Valuable Resource.

One characteristic that sets adults apart from younger learners is the vast wealth of experience that they have accumulated over the years. While they may have limited experience with the topic you are teaching, they nonetheless can often make connections from past experiences in order to help them learn new material. As you will see, learners' experience is one of the most important ideas that we will discuss in this book, and we will return to it time and again in the following chapters.

TIPS: *Use the learners' experience as a way to break the ice with a new group. Ask about their previous experiences and even consider using an activity that will allow them to share their experiences. Sometimes giving learners a chance to draw from their experiences will help the entire class by putting a "real life" perspective on your topic. In doing so, you have the potential to engage the learners more fully because the content takes on a personal meaning for the learners.*

4. It Is Important to Recognize That Decisions You Make About How You Will Teach Are Based on Whether You Are Trying to Change Attitudes and Values, Skills and Performance, or Knowledge and Factual Information.

Certain teaching techniques work better depending on what you are trying to achieve. For example, if you need to convey a lot of information in a short time, then a lecture is probably the most efficient way to reach the learners. But if you are trying to teach skills, various "hands-on" techniques like demonstration or simulation will engage the learners more directly. Finally, if you are trying to address topics that connect with learners' values, attitudes, or feelings, then techniques like discussion, role playing, and critical incidents will help adults learn more effectively than content-centered techniques will.

TIPS: *Make sure that you are clear about what you hope to accomplish and communicate this clearly to the learners. If they are expecting to learn practical skills, they may not respond well to long lectures. It is important to know and use a variety of teaching techniques, so that you can adapt what you do to what you are trying to accomplish.*

5. Most Adult Learning Is Self-Directed.

Research has shown that 70 percent or more of all learning is self-directed, which means it is planned, carried out, and evaluated primarily by the learner. This does not mean that we, as educators, have nothing to do with all of these learning activities. Rather, it means that the more we can do to encourage and support self-directedness in our learners, the more in harmony we will be with their urge toward self-direction.

TIPS: *While most adults have a certain level of readiness for self-direction, don't assume that the learners you work with will start out at a high level of self-direction. Levels of self-directedness will vary considerably among learners, but there are many strategies you can use to help learners become more self-directed. We will discuss these in the next chapter.*

6. The Need for Adult Learning Is Often Triggered by Some Kind of Developmental Transition or Crisis.

Quite often, adults will seek out learning opportunities when they experience some sort of change or crisis in their lives. Losing a job, being diagnosed with a chronic illness, becoming a parent, and ending a relationship with a spouse or partner are all examples of situations that might lead a person to seek out a learning opportunity. When I was diagnosed with Type II diabetes in 1995, I began a learning project consisting of individual education/counseling sessions, classes, and self-directed learning activities related to understanding and managing my diabetes; many of these continue to this day.

TIPS: *You will probably find it helpful to spend some time studying adult development theories and concepts. An understanding of the life cycle and the kinds of developmental transitions adults face can sometimes help you better understand the motives of your learners. Remember that empathy, authenticity, and respect, which were discussed in Chapter Two, involve getting to know the learner and trying to understand the whole person.*

7. Adults Choose to Learn for Many Different Reasons, and You Need to Know What These Are.

In a classic study from 1961, Cyril Houle asked a group of adults about the motives behind their decision to engage in learning. Basically, he found that the learners fell into three groups: (1) *Goal-oriented learners* had a clear purpose in mind and thought of their participation in learning as a means to some other end, like a promotion, a career change, or a new skill that they could use; (2) *Activity-oriented learners* had very different motives. These learners became involved in a course or other type of learning because they enjoyed the activity itself, and they were mainly interested in meeting and interacting with others; (3) *Learning-oriented learners* were those who participated simply for the sake of learning. These are the people Houle described as having an "inquiring mind." They are the people who sign up for classes just for fun or because it sounds interesting. They also take on a large number of self-directed learning projects on things that interest them in any given year.

Of course, there are other motives for participating in adult learning. Some of these include a requirement or expectation from others, the desire to contribute to the community or to promote social change, and even the hope of meeting a potential spouse or partner.

TIPS: *While it is not always possible to know why someone has enrolled in your class, any information you can find about this will be helpful. If you know why learners are there, you can target your approach to better meeting their needs. For example, if you know that your participants are required to be there, you can anticipate that you may encounter some resistance. If they are there to meet a specific goal, you can help them become clearer about the goal and how they can best attain it. And if you know that some of the learners are there for social reasons, you can decide whether you wish to provide time and activities for socialization.*

8. It Is Important to Understand Something About Motivation and How You Can Use Motivation Strategies to Help Excite the Learners About What You Are Teaching and, in Some Cases, to Help Break Down Learner Resistance.

Motivation is a tricky topic because we can't see it or touch it; we can only assume it is there and can *infer* it through different kinds of assessment. Yet a basic understanding of motivation will serve you well in knowing how best to meet the needs of your learners.

TIPS: *Knowing what motivates your learners can help you find ways to best evaluate whether they have learned successfully. If you know that they are motivated by external rewards, you can set up a schedule of reinforcements. But if the motivation is intrinsic, you can help learners decide how and when they have learned and help them see the inherent value of what they have learned. We will look more closely at motivation in Chapter Eleven.*

9. Teachers of Adults Need to Understand the Many Kinds of Barriers That Can Limit Whether Adults Choose a Learning Activity or Stay with the Activity.

Many factors can keep adults from registering for or remaining in a learning activity. Many of these barriers have to do with *situational* factors or life circumstances, such as lack of time or money, health problems, work obligations, or lack of childcare. Other barriers have to do with *institutional* policies or practices that can limit adult participation. These include not scheduling courses at a convenient time (for instance, older adults typically do not like to go out at night, so a senior center is likely to have a better turnout if they schedule a genealogy class during the daytime), lack of support services (such as financial aid, bookstore hours, parking), and not providing adequate information to the target audience. Finally, many barriers have to do with *dispositional*, or attitudinal, factors. We know that adults are often scared and lack confidence when they first return to the classroom (for example, students in "Adult Basic Education" often face fears related to their previous negative experiences with schooling).

TIPS: *Sometimes, barriers will be beyond your control. Life circumstances or institutional policies may keep a person from enrolling in your class. But when the learners do overcome these barriers, it is important for you to do things that will keep them there. A welcoming attitude, a supportive climate, and an approach that helps build confidence and shows that the person can learn will go a long way toward increasing retention of participants.*

10. Understanding Learning Style Is Important, but It Is Often Misunderstood and Misused.

I know you know this, but adults learn in different ways. There are many, many ways of defining and measuring learning styles, and each has certain strengths and limitations. In my view, it is fine to use learning style information to get a better understanding of individual learners. It is easy to misuse learning styles data, though, when teachers try to gather data and then adjust their classes in order to "teach to" the different styles. Its not as simple as "plug and play" to match styles with instruction, because the range of styles among your learners will vary considerably.

TIPS: *I suggest that you not reject learning styles information outright, but be careful not to oversimplify something complex by trying to be all things to all people. It's just not possible to do this. Rather, use learning styles information as a way to assess individuals and to help them find ways to maximize their own self-directed learning efforts. This can happen best in a climate in which learners are encouraged to support one another.*

11. Most Successful Adult Learning Takes Place in a Collaborative or Cooperative Setting, Where Sharing and Synergy Are Crucial.

This is the question of climate. What kind of a learning climate do you want to create? In my seven words for "teacher," I emphasized the importance of trust and respect. It is vital to be able to trust that one can share ideas or perspectives without being attacked or humiliated by other students or by the teacher. Respect means that it is important to value differences among the learners in your class. In essence, the classroom needs to be a "safe" space where learners can explore and "try on" different perspectives without fear of reprisal from others.

TIPS: *Tell learners right up front what kind of learning climate you are striving to achieve. Make it clear that you believe the greatest chance for success in learning will come when group members work together and support one another. This does not mean that students can't disagree with or challenge each other. It does mean, however, that this must be done in a way that respects and values the person.*

12. The Ultimate Purpose of Adult Education Is to Help Learners Think for Themselves.

Many years ago, I was on a panel at a research conference sitting next to Jack Mezirow, a highly respected professor of adult education (now retired) at Teachers College, Columbia University. When he said this, it really resonated with me. It wasn't a new or original idea; it is something very basic in the world of adult learning. But when he said it, at that moment, in that context, that was a "teachable moment" for me. I believe that it is the essence of everything discussed in this chapter.

TIPS: *Remember that it's all about the learner. As teachers, we are there to provide information, facilitate learning and change, train people in new skills, or help people generate solutions to the problems they have identified. But we are only a means to help people learn. Ultimately, success is determined by how well the learner achieves what he or she has set out to learn. We are only with our learners for a short time, but if we can convey the idea of "thinking for yourself," then we have taught something far more profound than any content that we are teaching.*

These twelve points are only a brief introduction to the exciting world of adult learning. Many books provide much more information about these and many other topics. Among these are *Adult Learning: Linking Theory and Practice* by Sharan B. Merriam and Laura L. Bierma; *Learning in Adulthood* (3rd ed.) by

Merriam, Caffarella, and Baumgartner; *How We Learn* by Knud Illeris; and *Transformative Learning in Practice* by Mezirow, Taylor, and Associates. Next, we are going to look at two more essential themes in adult learning—andragogy and self-directed learning.

THINK ABOUT IT

Identify and interview five adults about their activities as adult learners. You can choose family, friends, co-workers, or fellow students. Plan to spend about a half hour with them. Ask them the following:

- How many different learning activities did you engage in over the past year?
- What were the topics you studied?
- Were the activities primarily self-directed, or did you enroll in some sort of class, workshop, or training program?
- How many of your projects were related to work? To personal interests or hobbies? To dealing with issues going on in your life?
- How do you believe you learn best?

Jot down some notes and compare these. Do you see any trends among the learners? How about differences?

I use this activity when I teach my "Adult Learning" graduate class. The purpose is to give each person a chance to see how widespread learning is in most people's lives. Over the years, my students have been surprised by the responses they have received, especially from friends and relatives whom they know well.

Further Reading

Bjorklund, B.R. (2014). *The journey of adulthood* (8th ed.). Boston, MA: Pearson.

Houle, C.O. (1988). *The inquiring mind* (3rd ed.). Norman, OK: Oklahoma Research Center for Continuing Higher and Professional Education. (Originally published in 1961.)

Illeris, K. (2007). *How we learn*. London and New York: Routledge.

Knowles, M.S., Holton, E.F., III, & Swanson, R.A. (2011). *The adult learner*. Oxford, UK: Taylor & Francis.

Merriam, S.B., & Bierma, L.L. (2013). *Adult learning: Linking theory and practice*. San Francisco, CA: Jossey-Bass.

Merriam, S.B., Caffarella, R.S., & Baumgartner, L.M. (2007). *Learning in adulthood* (3rd ed.). San Francisco, CA: Jossey-Bass.

Mezirow, J., Taylor, E.W., & Associates. (2009). *Transformative learning in practice*. San Francisco, CA: Jossey-Bass.

5

BUILDING BLOCKS OF ADULT LEARNING

Like most fields, adult education and adult learning have numerous concepts, theories, and research findings designed to explain what we do and why we do it. The dozen points in the previous chapter have emerged from existing theory and research. Yet, there are certain concepts that are worthy of further discussion because they can be especially helpful to you in creating your own approach to teaching adults. In this chapter, I would like to introduce two concepts that are central to an understanding of adult learning and, in fact, are building blocks upon which much adult learning theory and practice have been built. These concepts are *andragogy* and *self-directed learning*.

Andra ... What?

Every field has its own unique jargon, and adult education is no exception. The word *andragogy* was probably used for the first time in Germany in the early 1800s. It literally means teaching (agog) of man (aner), or people. The term was popularized in the late 1960s and early 1970s by Malcolm Knowles, one of the most influential leaders in the world of adult education for many decades.

Knowles was interested in finding a way to identify some of the unique aspects of adult learning and, originally, to show differences between best practices for working with adults as opposed to working with children. He used andragogy as a way of contrasting with the better-known term *pedagogy*, which he described as a more traditional approach to teaching, usually used with children.

Over time, however, it became clear that there are times when andragogy can, in fact, be used effectively with children and times when pedagogy will work best with adults. Eventually, andragogy came to be viewed as less connected to age and more to one's maturity, experience, or sophistication in what one is studying.

So what is andragogy? For our purposes, *andragogy is a set of assumptions or best practices about how to work effectively with adult learners.* As stated above, andragogy need not be limited to adults, but for our purposes in this book, we are going to focus on adults.

Assumptions of Andragogy

Basically, andragogy involves *six* assumptions about how to help adult learners, as they mature in their knowledge and experience in a topic, gain the most from a learning activity. If a teacher follows and uses these assumptions, the chances of success for reaching the learner will multiply. Here, then, are the six assumptions of andragogy.

1. Need to Know

Whereas Younger Learners Are More Likely to Ask "What Do I Need to Know?," Adults Will More Often Ask "Why Do I Need to Know It?" Adult learners need to be shown *why* something is important to learn. If you are teaching art, adult learners may question why you shouldn't use acrylic paint on top of oil paint. For younger or novice learners, it might be enough just to know that you shouldn't do it.

2. Self-Concept

An Important Part of Maturity Is a Shift in Self-Concept from Being Dependent on Others Toward Becoming Increasingly Self-Directed. As learners begin to develop confidence, they are likely to become less dependent on the instructor and more self-directed. We will go into self-directed learning in the next section, but for now, just think of a person who is developing confidence about a topic and beginning to ask questions and apply the knowledge. Its like a bird spreading its wings for the first time and flying. And it's a great, empowering feeling for the learner that often makes her want to learn even more.

3. Learners' Experience

In Pedagogy, Learners Are Often Thought of as an "Empty Vessel" Waiting to Be Filled with Knowledge. In andragogy, experience is an important resource that helps learners make connections to their own lives and helps show that learners are likely to know much more about a topic than they may have thought. The point here is that, most of the time, the instructor is not the only one who knows something about the topic. If you can tap into the experience of your learners, you will find that you have a wonderful resource that will help you connect with the learners and increase their belief that they can learn.

4. Readiness to Learn

Whereas Children Are Required to Attend Compulsory Schooling, Adults Usually Decide When They Are Ready to Learn. Most often, adults decide to undertake a learning activity when they have decided that they *need* or *want* to learn something. It's something they have *chosen*, and they make this choice when they are *ready* to do so. A caveat here: in many professions and in most workplaces, there are times when people have to engage in learning in order to meet a requirement, such as professional certification or a job requirement about safety training, for example. So sometimes this one can be a little tricky; but for the most part, keep in mind that your learners are there because they *want* to be there. This should help boost your own confidence!

5. Orientation to Learning

Adults Most Often Undertake Learning in Order to Solve an Immediate Problem. Learners in formal school settings most often spend their time studying "subjects" like history, math, literature, or science. But the kinds of problems and challenges that adult learners face often cut across the boundaries of a single field of study. When I lived in upstate New York and was fascinated with learning about the Erie Canal, my "content" cut across fields as diverse as history, literature, music, photography, art, sociology, geography, and even engineering and architecture. I don't claim to be an expert in any of those areas, but to learn about the Canal and its place in history, I found myself learning about things from each of these disciplines. Again, the emphasis here is that adults learn most often in order to solve a problem of concern to them in the here and now.

6. Motivation

In Andragogy, We Assume That, Most of the Time, Motivation Is Intrinsic (That Is, It Comes from Within the Person), Rather Than Extrinsic (Coming from Rewards and Punishment from Others). To be sure, there are times when adults are motivated by outside factors, such as career advancement, receiving a raise, or managing a chronic health problem, but for the most part, the motivation to learn comes from something inside the person, such as curiosity, satisfaction, the desire to achieve a goal, or the confidence that one can learn successfully. We will look more closely at motivation in Chapter Eleven.

To simplify, when adopting principles of andragogy, a teacher of adults is most likely to:

- Help the learners understand why they are learning and not just what they will be learning;

- Assist learners to develop knowledge, skills, and attitudes that will help make them more ready to take a role in directing their own learning;
- Draw from learners' experiences in a way that helps them connect to the topic from what they have learned or experienced in the past;
- Understand that, most of the time, adults will be more successful if they recognize they need to learn something and are *ready* to do so;
- Take steps to ensure that what is being taught is practical in helping learners to solve the problems that brought them to the setting in the first place; and
- Encourage learners to look inward in order to see the value of investing in the learning activity.

This is the essence of andragogy!

We will touch on principles of andragogy from time to time as we move through the book. For now, keep in mind that, even though there has been considerable debate over whether andragogy is a theory, a conceptual framework, or a set of assumptions, for our purposes, andragogy is simply a set of "best practices" designed to lead to successful adult learning.

Self-Directed Learning

It has been more than forty years since Allen Tough, a Canadian educator from the University of Toronto, published his classic work, *The Adult's Learning Projects*. In this book, Tough found that adults participate in an average of eight different learning projects in a given year. Tough described adult learning as an iceberg, where the vast majority of learning activity lies beneath the surface, not readily visible to educators. He found that almost 70 percent of all learning activities were planned, implemented, and evaluated primarily by the learners themselves. This one study opened the floodgates of research on what has become one of the most widely studied topics in adult education since the early 1970s.

For teachers of adults, the research on self-directed learning (SDL) has profound implications. If we know that the vast majority of adult learning is self-directed, then it only makes sense that, if we want to connect more effectively with our learners, we need to understand this important approach to how they most often engage in learning projects or activities. As a teacher, if you can understand and draw from what we know about successful SDL, you can use this knowledge to create learning activities that are more in harmony with the most natural and frequent way in which adults approach their learning. Here, I am not saying that you should try to *replace* learner's self-directed efforts with more formal education; rather, it's about creating a harmony between a learner's tendency toward self-direction and your own teaching.

In this section, I will introduce you to the concept of self-directed learning. Then I will present a few myths and misunderstandings about SDL and how an understanding of these can help you implement SDL principles into your own teaching without "losing control" of your class. Finally, I will share a checklist, developed by Roger Hiemstra, of ways in which you can incorporate aspects of SDL into your teaching, even if you are teaching highly prescribed mandatory content, such as safety in the workplace.

Unlocking the Mystery of Self-Directed Learning

Self-directed learning is something of a mystery because, as Tough has shown, it lies beneath the surface and is not easily visible. Yet, like an iceberg, the part that lies beneath the surface is by far more encompassing than the tip that can be seen above the surface.

There are many definitions of self-directed learning. Roger Hiemstra and I, in our 1991 book *Self-Direction in Adult Learning: Perspectives on Theory, Research, and Practice*, have offered this textbook definition of SDL: "self-direction in learning refers to both the external characteristics of an instructional process and the internal characteristics of the learner, where the individual assumes primary responsibility for a learning experience" (p. 24). In other words, when we speak of self-directed learning, we need to distinguish between a teaching-learning process whereby individuals are in charge of the process and the notion that self-direction is a personal, psychological characteristic that contributes to our ability to be self-directed in learning as well as in life in general.

Although research on SDL has only emerged since the 1970s, the idea of learners taking charge of their learning can be found throughout history. Early examples include the Greek philosophers Socrates, Aristotle, and Plato, along with Alexander the Great, Erasmus of Rotterdam, and Descartes. Self-directed learning was particularly important in Colonial America. Benjamin Franklin stands out as an obvious example. In more recent times, we see examples of successful self-directed learners in such luminaries as Frank Lloyd Wright, Amelia Earhart, Harry Truman, Malcolm X, Walt Disney, and Virginia Woolf. These people were highly successful, but had no formal education beyond high school.

As one more example, Lorraine Cavaliere studied the process by which the Wright Brothers invented the airplane. She described how this process took place over many years, with numerous fits and starts, small gains and setbacks. But they persisted and, through a process that was mostly self-directed, achieved success on December 3, 1903, at Kitty Hawk, North Carolina.

My point is that self-directed learning is not merely a current fad, but is an idea rooted in history. However, as we are gaining a greater understanding of SDL, we can use it to better serve our learners.

What You Need to Know About Self-Directed Learning

It is not my intention in this book to present a major treatise on SDL; rather I would like to share a few key ideas that you can use immediately to tap into the self-directedness of your learners and to help them become increasingly self-directed in the process. Here are a few things that you need to know about SDL.

1. *We all have different levels of readiness for self-direction.* SDL is not an "all or nothing" concept that you either have or do not have. Rather, some degree of self-direction exists in each of us. Our self-directedness is influenced by many things, including past experiences with learning, our personality and psychological makeup, and the setting and classroom environment, among others. As Knowles pointed out, in andragogy, it is important to help learners become more and more self-directed.

2. *Promoting self-direction in the classroom does not eliminate the role of the facilitator.* In fact, just the opposite holds true. It is a myth that, when encouraging self-direction, anything goes and the teacher just sits back and lets the learners "have at it." Instead, the facilitator of SDL is an *active* part of the process. Facilitating SDL means negotiating goals and learning strategies, serving as an expert resource, guiding the process, and helping learners determine when they have met their goals. The importance of the teacher is not lost in SDL; instead, what changes is the *role* of the teacher—from content expert and main provider of information to facilitator of the learning process and expert resource.

3. *Self-directed learning does not always take place in isolation.* We often think of self-directed learners being on their own, learning in isolation. Sometimes this is true, but most often SDL is an active process that involves interacting with others. Sometimes self-directed learners are most successful when they are working with a community of like-minded

folks who share their interests. A truly insightful self-directed learner knows when to turn to someone with more knowledge on the topic in order to gain new skills or insights. This is why using principles of self-direction in a classroom setting makes sense. It does not "undo" the spirit of the classroom; rather, it makes the classroom a more lively, active setting for learning to take place.

4. *Self-directed learning requires a certain amount of "up-front" time to help the learners understand the process and to "try out" new skills.* Instructors who wish to implement self-directed learning strategies must keep in mind that this doesn't just happen by itself. If you are working with learners who are used to a traditional class setting where they take on a passive role, you need to take some time to build trust, develop confidence, and show learners the value of engaging in a self-directed process. Some learners are quite naturally going to resist. These individuals may fear the unknown, or they may simply not want to extend the effort it takes to control their learning. In any case, this is where the instructor needs to shift into a facilitator role and clearly show the benefits of engaging in SDL. As I have said elsewhere, this is where it's important to *trust the process.*

5. *More than four decades of research supports the importance of self-direction as important for all learners, but especially adults.* Tough's work set in motion a whole body of research. Numerous replications of his original study basically supported his finding that nearly 70 percent of all adult learning is self-directed. Eventually, newer and more sophisticated research instruments and methods added further to our understanding. Today we have evidence that self-directedness is related to a host of variables. Some of these include self-concept, creativity, resilience, previous education, life satisfaction, wellness, and cross-cultural adaptability.

Putting Self-Directed Learning into Practice

Many writers have discussed how to implement self-directed learning in the educational environment. One of the best resources today is a long-out-of-print book by Malcolm Knowles entitled *Self-Directed Learning: A Guide for Teachers and Learners*. It can still be found in libraries and on the Internet and is worth the investment.

Another guide that can help teachers put self-directed learning principles into practice was devised by my friend and colleague Roger Hiemstra. Recognizing that certain institutional policies or specific training guidelines may limit how much control it is possible to give the learner, Roger came up with a list of what he calls "micro components" of self-directed learning. These are decision points at various stages in the planning process where it might be possible to give learners a certain amount of control. For example, if you are working in a training setting where there is a set curriculum and a test that must be passed in order for workers to be certified, there are limited opportunities for self-directed learning. However, there *will* be elements of the process where you can give choices to the learners. The micro components will allow you to identify those decision points at which you can promote elements of self-direction, regardless of the outside forces that may impact the teaching-learning process. The micro components of self-directed learning are presented in Exhibit 5.1.

EXHIBIT 5.1. Roger Hiemstra's Micro Components of Self-Directed Learning.

1. Assessing Needs

    1.1. Choice of individual techniques

    1.2. Choice of group techniques

    1.3. Controlling how needs information is reported

    1.4. Controlling how needs information is used

2. Setting goals

    2.1. Specifying objectives

    2.2. Determining the nature of the learning

    2.2.1. Deciding on competency or mastery learning-vs.-pleasure or interest learning

    2.2.2. Deciding on the types of questions to be asked and

answered during learning efforts

2.2.3. Determining emphases to be placed on the application of the knowledge or skill acquired

2.3. Changing ("evolution") objectives over the period of a learning experience

2.4. Use of learning contracts

2.4.1. Making various learning choices or selecting from various options

2.4.2. Decisions on how to achieve objectives

3. Specifying learning content
   3.1. Decisions on adjusting levels of difficulty
   3.2. Controlling sequence of learning material
   3.3. Choices on knowledge types (psychomotor, cognition, affective)
   3.4. Decision on theory-vs.-practice or application
   3.5. Deciding on level of competency
   3.6. Decisions on actual content
   3.6.1. Choices on financial or other costs involved in the learning effort
   3.6.2. Deciding on the help, resources, or experiences required for the content

3.7. Prioritizing the learning content

3.8. Deciding on the major planning type, such as self, other learners, experts, etc.

4. Pacing the learning
   4.1. Amount of time devoted to teacher presentations
   4.2. Amount of time spent on teacher-to-learner interactions
   4.3. Amount of time spent on learner-to-learner interactions
   4.4. Amount of time spent on individualized learning activities
   4.5. Deciding on pace of movement through learning experiences
   4.6. Decisions on when to complete parts or all of the activities

5. Choosing the instructional methods, techniques, and devices
   5.1. Selection of options for technological support and instructional devices
   5.2. Choice of instructional method or technique
   5.3. Type of learning resources to be used
   5.4. Choice of learning modality (sight, sound, touch, etc.) for determining how best to learn

5.5. Choices on opportunities for learners, learner and teacher, small group, or large group discussion

6. Controlling the learning environment
   6.1. Decision on manipulating physical/environmental features
   6.2. Deciding to deal with emotional/psychological impediments
   6.3. Choices on ways to confront social/cultural barriers
   6.4. Opportunities to match personal learning style preferences with informational presentations

7. Promoting introspection, reflection, and critical thinking
   7.1. Deciding on means for interpreting theory
   7.2. Choices on means for reporting/recording critical reflections
   7.3. Decision on use of reflective practitioner techniques
   7.4. Opportunities provided for practicing decision-making, problem solving, and policy formulation
   7.5. Making opportunities to seek clarity or to clarify ideas available
   7.6. Choices on practical ways to apply new learning

8. Instructor's/trainer's role
   8.1. Choice of the role or nature of didactic (lecturing) presentations
   8.2. Choice of the role or nature of Socratic (questioning) techniques to be used
   8.3. Choice of the role or nature of facilitative (guiding the learning process) procedures

9. Evaluating the learning
   9.1. Choice on the use and type of testing
   9.1.1. Deciding on the nature and use of any reviewing
   9.1.2. Opportunities for practice testing available
   9.1.3. Opportunities for retesting available
   9.1.4. Opportunities available for choosing type of testing, if any, to be used
   9.1.5. Decisions on weight given to any test results
   9.2. Choices on type of feedback to be used
   9.2.1. Deciding on type of instructor's feedback to learner
   9.2.2. Deciding on type of learner's feedback to instructor
   9.3. Choices on means for validating achievements (learning)

9.4. Deciding on nature of learning outcomes

9.4.1. Choosing type of final products

9.4.1.1. Deciding how evidence of learning is reported or presented

9.4.1.2. Opportunities made available to revise and resubmit final products

9.4.1.3. Decisions on the nature of any written products

9.4.2. Decision on weight given to final products

9.4.3. Deciding on level of practicality of outcomes

9.4.3.1. Opportunities to relate learning to employment/future employment

9.4.3.2. Opportunities to propose knowledge application ideas

9.4.4. Deciding on nature of the benefits from any learning

9.4.4.1. Opportunities to propose immediate benefits versus long-term benefits

9.4.4.2. Opportunities to seek various types of benefits or acquisition of new skills

9.5. Deciding on the nature of any follow-up evaluation

9.5.1. Determining how knowledge can be maintained over time

9.5.2. Determining how concepts are applied

9.5.3. Opportunities provided to review or redo material

9.5.4. Follow-up or spin-off learning choices

9.6. Opportunities made available to exit learning experience and return later if appropriate

9.7. Decision on the type of grading used or completion rewards to be received

9.8. Choosing the nature of any evaluation of instructor and learning experience

9.9. Choices on the use and/or type of learning contracts

9.7. Decision on the type of grading used or completion rewards to be received

9.8. Choosing the nature of any evaluation of instructor and learning experience

9.9. Choices on the use and/or type of learning contracts

From: R. Hiemstra (1994). Helping learners take responsibility for self-directed activities (pp. 81–87). In R. Hiemstra & R.G. Brockett (Eds.), *Overcoming resistance to self-direction in learning.* New Directions for Adult and Continuing Education No. 64. San Francisco, CA: Jossey-Bass. Reproduced by permission.

Conclusion

This chapter was designed to provide a foundation for an under-standing about two central concepts in adult learning. The intent was to introduce you to the value of linking andragogy and self-directed learning principles and practices into your teaching. As you can see, the connection is a natural one that is consistent with how most adults go about their own learning and, thus, can lead to important outcomes for the learner. Perhaps most impor-tant is that, if learners are able to assume greater control over the teaching-learning process, they will be more motivated to learn and will want to continue learning long after your course has ended. Andragogy and self-directed learning can contribute to this.

THINK ABOUT IT

A. Think about a learning project you have undertaken in the last year or two.

1. Were you more concerned with *why* you were learning than with *what* you were learning? Was the instructor clear about explaining *why* you were learning about this topic?

2. To what extent were you self-directed in this learning activity? What did the teacher do to encourage or limit opportunities for self-direction?

3. Was your past experience helpful to you in undertaking the learning project? To what extent did the instructor tap into your experience?

4. To what extent was the decision to undertake the learning project yours? Was there pressure from others to participate, or were you fulfilling a requirement by engaging in the learning?

5. Did you undertake the project in order to try to solve a problem in your work or personal life? Did the content of your learning project come from more than one field?

6. How much of the motivation to participate in the learning project came from within you? How much was the motivation influenced by outside factors such as possible rewards?

   Now reflect for a moment on your responses. To what extent do you believe that you were practicing the assumptions of andragogy? Did you make conscious decisions about the ideas in the above questions? If you were in a setting with an instructor or facilitator, to what degree did she practice or encourage the above principles of teaching? Might it have changed the learning experience if the instructor had taken a different approach (more learner-centered OR more teacher-directed)?

B. Think back on a time when you were involved in a learning project where you made all or most of the decisions about what you wanted to learn, how you wanted to learn it, and when you would be satisfied that you had learned. Why did you choose to engage in self-directed learning? How did you feel as you were going through the learning activity? How well do you believe you accomplished your goals?

Now think about where you are currently teaching or where you hope to teach in the near future. What are some of the factors that would make it desirable to implement elements of SDL? What forces might limit your opportunities to do so? What can you do to ensure that learners will leave your class with a willingness to continue learning on their own afterward?

Further Reading

Brockett, R.G., & Hiemstra, R. (1991). *Self-direction in adult learning: Perspectives on theory, research, and practice.* London and New York: Routledge.

Knowles, M.S. (1975). *Self-directed learning: A guide for teachers and learners.* New York: Association Press.

Knowles, M.S. (1980). *The modern practice of adult education* (rev. ed.). New York: Cambridge.

Tough, A. (1979). *The adult's learning projects* (2nd ed.). Austin, TX: Learning Concepts.

6

PLANNING INSTRUCTION

In the previous two chapters, we concentrated on the need to know about characteristics of adult learners. For the next two chapters, and again in the four chapters of Part Three, attention will shift to **the need to know about teaching and the instructional process**. We will begin this discussion of teaching with a look at how to create a class session or an entire course. This is the process of planning instruction.

Ever since Ralph Tyler published his *Basic Principles of Curriculum and Instruction* in 1949, educators from across all levels have worked to develop models that can be used to plan and evaluate instruction. Some are comprised of a few basic steps, and others are very complex with numerous steps and even sub-steps in the process. Tyler was mainly interested in curriculum at the K–12 level; however, adult educators, trainers, and instructional designers, among others, have used this basic process as a starting point to better understand how to use similar principles with adult learners.

In this chapter, I would like to introduce a very basic planning process consisting of four steps you will need to consider when developing a lesson or a course for adults: *purpose, plan, implement,* and *evaluate.* I realize that, for more experienced teachers, this material is likely to be "old hat"; if so, you might want to jump ahead to the next chapter. However, I include it here for those readers who have not been exposed to a planning process. But before we look at the steps in the process, I need to share five important caveats about planning and evaluation:

1. Planning and evaluation can refer to an *individual session* or to an *entire course*. In this chapter, we will look at examples of both approaches.

2. Some planning models are very complex with multiple steps and sub-steps; others, like the one in this chapter, are designed to focus on the main steps in the process.

3. In the past, most planning models have been described as a linear set of steps that should be followed in sequence. However, more recent models are often circular with numerous feedback loops and may not be as prescriptive as more traditional models. The approach I am using here is not my own, but rather an amalgam of approaches. For instance, it is similar in some ways to, but different from, models presented by Tyler and by Knowles, Holton, and Swanson. It is linear because it should help you to move sequentially through the planning process; yet, I encourage you to keep in mind that planning is not always an orderly process. Remember that there will be times when you need to revisit something from an earlier stage or skip over an aspect of the level you are working on and come back to it later.

4. Planning and evaluation models are not limited to adult learning situations. Much of what we discuss in this chapter is similar to what is typically used in K–12 and higher education settings. It is based on general principles of instructional development. However, the examples in this chapter are drawn specifically from adult learning situations.

5. Finally, in the model I present, I am assuming that the need for instruction has already been established and that the decision to offer the program has already been made and supported. For example, a group of people may have approached the dean of Continuing Education at the local community

college asking for a course on strategies for financing a home in difficult economic times. Therefore, I am deliberately skipping over the important topic of needs assessment for our purposes in this book.

Purpose

A good instructional plan begins with a well-defined sense of purpose. You will need to have a clear idea of (1) what you are hoping to achieve and (2) specifically what learners will be expected to know in order to determine that the purpose has been met. This is where you will need to set goals and objectives for the program or course. Goals reflect the overall purpose, whereas objectives are the steps that enable learners to meet the goal.

One key question in developing the purpose is whether you need to have outcomes that are directly measurable. Many training programs require that participants pass a program with a certain test score. For example, the GED test, which measures high school equivalency, is based on learners receiving a predetermined passing score. In such cases, objectives may be worded with very specific outcomes, such as:

Participants will be able to perform the procedure in less than four minutes, with a minimum score of 75.

In most cases, however, the goal will be much more general and not tied to specific measurable objectives. For example, in a class on Italian cooking, the purpose may simply be stated as: "In this class, participants will have fun learning new ways to prepare Italian cuisine. We will learn to prepare an appetizer, a main course, and a dessert."

In my graduate classes, I usually tie my objectives to the overall purpose in terms of what I call "proficiencies," which are more general indicators of learning and are not usually quantifiable. In Exhibit 6.1, I share an example of proficiencies for a graduate class on teaching adults:

EXHIBIT 6.1. **Ralph's List of Proficiencies for a Course on Teaching Adults.**

At the completion of the course, given active participation, each individual should be able to do the following:

1. Assess personal strengths and weaknesses as a teacher of adults;

2. Describe one's personal style as a teacher of adults;

3. Identify and describe several elements of effective teaching;

4. Select methods and techniques most appropriate for the type of learning outcomes to be met in a particular situation;

5. Understand several ways in which the instructional process can be tailored to individual needs of learners;

6. Identify roles and responsibilities of teachers who work with adults;

7. Develop one's understanding of and skill with using a wide range of methods and techniques; and

8. Demonstrate an ability to successfully use at least one method or technique.

You will note that each of these proficiencies is worded in a way that can be demonstrated; however, they cannot be measured quantitatively. I usually ask learners to use these proficiencies as a self-assessment tool. My evaluation of the students' work is based on their performance on several learning activities throughout the course that reflect these proficiencies.

One final consideration when trying to determine goals and objectives is the need to set priorities in terms of what is most important to include. This can be done by breaking content down according to what is (1) essential to know; (2) important to know; and (3) nice to know. While you will probably want to include some of each of these in your course, I suggest you prioritize your content and then cover material in each category in a proportional way (that is, more time spent on what is essential and less time spent on what is nice to know).

Plan

Once you have determined your overall goal and the objectives that will enable learners to meet the goal, the next step is to actually plan your class session or course. Basically, this is where you make decisions about what to include and how to cover it.

Here, the idea is to use the goal and objectives in order to determine how best to achieve them. This is where you will make decisions about what content to cover, which techniques to use, and what criteria will be used to determine how well learners have achieved the goals.

In the planning stage you will be making decisions about what material to cover and how to sequence it, moving from basic content to more specific advanced areas. You will have to determine *how much* you can cover during the allotted time. Good planning means knowing how much to include in order to hold the learners' attention without overwhelming them. It's a delicate balance, but don't worry, it will come to you over time. When we reach the evaluation process, there are ways to obtain feedback to help you figure this out for future courses.

The planning stage is also where you will make decisions about course requirements. If you are teaching a non-credit course like financial planning or a gardening class, you will want to make sure that learners are clear about what they will "take away" from the class; at the same time, you won't need to be concerned about having learners submit assignments (sometimes known as "deliverables," especially in the training/human resources world). On the other hand, if you are teaching adults in a credit course, you will be expected to make assignments so that you can assess performance, often to assign a grade.

Once decisions have been made about course content and requirements, the planning process shifts to dealing with logistics. Here is where practical steps, such as ordering books and materials, developing a syllabus and handouts, and creating a schedule, are handled. You may also need to develop and disseminate promotional materials to help you advertize your class.

A final planning decision has to do with whether you wish to contact learners prior to the class. In the past, it was most common to receive a list of participants shortly before the beginning of class and to meet them when they walked through the door at the first session. However, in today's world, with electronic communication and tools that make it possible to contact learners several weeks in advance of the course, the game is changed. It is now possible to send emails to "welcome" the learners, share information about the course, announce the required books and reading assignments so readers can be prepared before the class, and even make brief assignments prior to the first class. In other words, the class may in fact begin some time before the first official meeting. It is important to not exploit the process and bombard students with information or assignments before you actually meet with them. But if they have had contact before they walk into the room, it can be a good way to begin building rapport and setting the stage for your class.

Implement

Ok, so you have determined your goals and objectives and come up with a plan for the program. Now its time to make it happen. The implementation stage is where you put the plan into effect or "work the plan." This phase is exciting because it's where the hard work pays off. Now you are with the learners, using the activities and assignments you have created in order to help them learn about the topic.

I'm not going to say a lot about implementation here, because it is covered directly in many of the other chapters. Remember the seven characteristics and the four elements of effective teaching (Chapter Two). Also, remember what you have learned about adult learners (Chapters Four and Five). In the next four chapters, we will cover several important aspects related to implementation: teaching techniques, the learning environment, overcoming resistance to learning, and motivation.

Evaluate

Although listed last in the planning process, evaluation should take place *throughout* the entire teaching-learning process. We need to distinguish between *two* types of evaluation, and both are very important. *Formative* evaluation centers on evaluating the process. It is ongoing and is used to give feedback in order to *improve* the course or program. Sometimes, formative evaluation can be as simple as asking learners for written comments about what they liked best and least during a class session. Don't ask them to sign their names. You can use these brief reviews to see what participants thought went well and what they thought could have been done differently. Formative evaluation can be used throughout a course as a way of making sure you and the learners are on the same page, and to make adjustments when needed.

Formative evaluation can also be used to give feedback to the learners at different points during the course. Rather than waiting for a final evaluation at the end of the course, formative evaluation can give learners an idea of their strengths and areas in which they need improvement in order to receive a strong final evaluation or grade. In non-credit courses, formative evaluation is valuable because it can help learners gain a feel for what they are doing well and where they need to make changes. For instance, in a piano class, an instructor can go around the room and give individuals tips for improvement as they are learning new songs or techniques.

Summative evaluation is what most often comes to mind when we think of evaluation. It is where learners are evaluated on their overall performance in a course or workshop. In credit classes, this is the course grade. In certificate training programs, it is the decision whether or not to award certification to a learner. The focus on summative evaluation is on *outcomes* or results. As you might expect, grading is very intimidating for most learners. This is especially true with adult learners who have been away from the classroom setting for many years. For this reason, it is important to make sure that you have been clear about the criteria for success in the course and that you have devised appropriate and fair ways to assess performance.

The other side of summative evaluation involves student evaluation of courses and instructors. Many universities and other educational providers require that instructors distribute a course/instructor evaluation at the end of the course. Here students have a chance to give feedback about the course. While these can and often are used for future course improvement, summative course evaluations are also used in decisions about promotion, tenure, merit, and even the decision to rehire a teacher. As an instructor, you want to know the criteria upon which you will be evaluated and, while I don't suggest that you teach in a way that will simply meet the items on the evaluation, you should be aware of what is generally expected.

Conclusion

Planning and evaluation are essential to effective teaching. They provide the foundation upon which your course, workshop, or class session is built. In this chapter, I have offered a brief introduction to planning and evaluation, knowing that, for some readers, this will be very general, while for others it will be brand new. If you would like to know more about instructional planning and evaluation, I suggest that you look at *Designing Instruction for Adult Learners* by Gary J. Dean and *Planning Programs for Adult Learners* by Rosemary S. Caffarella and Sandra Ratcliff Daffron. These books provide a more detailed look at the planning process than is possible in the brief overview offered in this chapter.

As a way of bringing the chapter to a close, I would like to leave you with some questions that can help guide your planning process. These are presented in Table 6.1.

Table 6.1 Questions to Consider in Planning and Evaluating Instruction for Adults

Step	Description
Purpose	What is the overall purpose of the course or the session? Is there a broad goal in mind? What objectives or proficiencies will be proposed in order to meet the goal? Is there an actual need for what is being planned?
Planning	What am I going to cover? How much time will I need for each topic? What are the best techniques to use to accomplish the objective? Am I going to ask learners to prepare anything beforehand (for example, readings or written activities)? Do I want to invite guest resources or use video or other media resources? What equipment or materials, if any, will I need?
Implementation	Have I prepared my content and reviewed it to make sure it's at an appropriate level for the class? Is the room set up as I want it to be? Do I have all of the equipment and materials I need to teach the session? Have I thought about what I want the learners to do during our time together? Are the techniques I have chosen the best way to meet the objective(s) for the session?
Evaluation	Do I understand the different purposes of formative and summative evaluation? What strategies do I believe could help me obtain feedback during the course? How often during the course would this kind of feedback be helpful? What kinds of activities or assignments can I use to provide ongoing feedback to the learners? How am I going to determine the extent to which goals and objectives have been met? If I am required to give a grade or other type of formal assessment, what criteria will I use? What can I do to assure that learners will be evaluated fairly and on the pre-established criteria? If my program requires an instructor evaluation, have I determined a process to administer evaluations in an anonymous and open way?

THINK ABOUT IT

Using a course or a specific lesson that you have taught in the past, go back and write a plan using the four steps described in this chapter. This plan can be a detailed list or just a basic outline of the major steps you need to cover.

As you look at your plan, think about which portions you included when you previously taught the course or lesson. Did any new questions come to mind as you have used the planning process? Did you come up with some ways to improve the teaching/learning process that you can use the next time you teach the lesson?

Further Reading

Caffarella, R.S., & Daffron, S.R. (2013). *Planning programs for adult learners* (3rd ed.). San Francisco, CA: Jossey-Bass.

Dean, G.J. (2002). *Designing instruction for adult learners* (2nd ed.). Malabar, FL: Krieger.

Hiemstra, R., & Sisco, B. (1990). *Individualizing instruction: Making learning personal, empowering, and successful.* San Francisco, CA: Jossey-Bass.

Knowles, M. (1980). *The modern practice of adult education* (rev. ed.). New York: Cambridge.

Silberman, M. (2006). *Active training* (3rd ed.). San Francisco, CA: Pfeiffer.

Spaulding, D. (2014). *How to teach adults: Plan your class, teach your students, change the world* (exp. ed.). San Francisco, CA: Jossey-Bass.

7

TEACHING TECHNIQUES

Now that you have an understanding of what goes into planning adult learning activities, what are you actually going to *do* once you are in front of the learners? What are you going to do in order to *implement* your plan? You have to decide which teaching techniques will best meet your objectives. Sounds simple, right? And it can be simple . . . except that you have to understand how and why to select certain techniques for different purposes. In this chapter, we will take a look at some things that need to be considered when selecting teaching techniques (sometimes also referred to as *methods*). Then I would like to introduce you to a few techniques you can use to start teaching adults.

Tips for Selecting Teaching Techniques

The following tips should be considered when deciding on which techniques to select in a given situation:

1. Use a variety of techniques. Don't always rely on the same approach, even though it may be tempting to stick with what is familiar to you.

2. According to Gary Dean, there are two important factors in selecting techniques. The first is whether learner involvement in the activity should be low, medium, or high. With some techniques, the learner is a passive recipient of information, while in others, active involvement is necessary for learning to take place. The second factor has to do with what

you are trying to teach. Is the focus on content, skills, or values and attitudes? Certain techniques will work best for each of these domains of learning. Likewise, in techniques that focus on presenting content, learners are often going to be less active than in skill-based or values-oriented activities.

3. Time is an important consideration in selecting techniques. Some techniques, such as certain structured experiences or in-basket exercises, may require more time to complete than others. If you have the time available and the topic is of sufficient importance to make it worthwhile, then go for it. But if time is limited, it might be better to look for a less time-intensive alternative.

4. As creatures of habit, most of us find it easier to turn to what feels comfortable and familiar. In my early years of teaching, my presentations were almost always filled with numerous overhead transparency slides. While this was fine for a while, eventually it became predictable and stale. I knew that I had to try something different. The suggestion I have is not to be afraid to stretch yourself and learn new techniques that at first may feel awkward and unfamiliar. I'm not suggesting you do a major overhaul at one time; rather, try working in a few new techniques from time to time. Keep the ones that work well and modify or get rid of the ones that don't work for you. Your learners will appreciate the change of pace that comes from doing something new and different!

5. Be sensitive to avoid using techniques that could be embarrassing or hurtful to learners. For example, an activity that involves sitting on the floor is perfectly appropriate for a Yoga class, and learners know to expect this when they sign up. But in a class on management techniques, asking participants to sit in a circle on the floor could be difficult or embarrassing for someone with limited mobility.

6. Stay on top of new developments in education and training in order to learn about techniques that may be helpful with

the topic you are teaching. With technology changing at such a rapid pace, this is essential. But there are new and exciting techniques in nearly all fields. As was mentioned in Chapter Three, staying on top of new developments in your field is an essential part of effective teaching. This means not only keeping abreast of your content area, but of teaching techniques as well.

Six Techniques to Help You Start

When you are trying to decide which techniques you will use in your instructional plan, you will be amazed by the actual number from which to choose. Exhibit 7.1 is a composite list from several different resources of techniques that can be used with adult learners. Remember, though, that this is only a partial list. Different names are often used for similar activities.

EXHIBIT 7.1. **A List of Teaching Techniques for Adults*.**

- Action Learning
- Apprenticeship
- Behavioral Modeling
- Blog
- Brain-Based Learning
- Brainstorming
- Buzz Groups
- Case Story
- Case Study
- Colloquy
- Computer-Aided Instruction
- Concept Maps
- Concrete Practice
- Conference
- Correspondence Study
- Critical Incident
- Critical Thinking Techniques
- Debate
- Demonstration
- Dialogue
- Discussion
- Exhibit
- Field Trip
- Fishbowl
- Forum
- Games
- Group Discussion
- Icebreaker Activities
- In-Basket Exercise
- Independent Study

*This list has been adapted from the following authors: Michael W. Galbraith, Gary J. Dean, Rosemary S. Caffarella and Sandra Ratcliff Daffron, Mel Silberman, and Sharon L. Bowman.

- Individualized Instruction
- Institute
- Interactive Lecture
- Interactive Media
- Internship
- Interview
- Jigsaw
- Learner-Created Games
- Learning Contracts
- Lecture
- Listening Teams
- Mental Imagery
- Mentoring
- Metaphor Analysis
- Microteaching
- Narrative Learning
- Newsletters
- Observation
- Nominal Group Technique
- Panel
- Participation Training
- Podcast
- Practice
- Psychodrama
- Quiet Meeting
- Reflective Practice
- Role Play
- Self-Directed Learning
- Simulation
- Skills-Based Activities
- Storytelling
- Structured Experience
- Teach-Back Activities
- Wiki
- Workshop

Overwhelming? You bet! Over the years I have used many of these techniques, but in all honesty there are some on the list about which I know very little. If you wish to learn more or try out some of these techniques, many books and Internet resources offer detailed information. Three resources I recommend for further information on different teaching techniques are *Adult Learning Methods* (3rd ed.), edited by Michael W. Galbraith, *Active Training* (3rd ed.) by Mel Silberman, and *Training from the Back of the Room* by Sharon L. Bowman. These books include tips and resources for using many of the techniques listed above.

For our purposes in this chapter, since the focus is on some basic techniques that you can use right away, I would like to share *six* different techniques—two each for learning content, skills, and attitudes. Once you are comfortable with these, I encourage you to expand your repertoire and try out more new techniques.

Techniques for Teaching Content

Content-based techniques are essential. These approaches allow you to reach any sized group and to cover a great deal of material in a short time. But despite the reputation they often have as being passive and sometimes boring, when used in conjunction with other approaches, they can be very engaging and lively techniques. The two techniques covered here are lecture and panel.

Lecture. At its most basic, a lecture involves passing on one's expertise to a group of learners who passively take in the knowledge, often by writing detailed notes about what has been said. It is, to be sure, the most basic and probably most common technique used when teaching adults. As you know, the success of a lecture has mainly to do with how interesting the topic is and whether the speaker is dynamic. We have all sat through lectures we thought would never end. I confess that I, too, have dozed off in lectures over the years. It was sometimes hard to stay awake during lectures in my 8 a.m. astronomy class held in the dimly lit planetarium. But a good lecture (or speech) can be informative, inspiring, and memorable. Look no further than Martin Luther King, Jr.'s "I Have a Dream" speech delivered at the Lincoln Memorial in 1963.

As an undergraduate, I took a social psychology class taught by a professor who had a lifelong stutter, which he acknowledged during the first class session. However, it quickly became clear that this professor knew how to grab and hold the attention of his class. He was an incredible storyteller and shared lessons about topics such as groupthink, prisoner's dilemma, and altruism by incorporating memorable stories from real life. The fact that the man stuttered throughout his lectures was quickly forgotten as his captivating stories unfolded. I looked forward to his class and even had a friend who was not enrolled in the class but sometimes sat in out of personal interest. This professor was able to turn something that could have been a debilitating limitation into a very real strength through the power of his storytelling and some very interesting content.

Here are a few ideas to keep in mind in order to make the most of your lectures:

- Try to keep lectures fairly brief. Two short lectures of 15 minutes interspersed with an activity will usually keep your group more engaged than one 30- or 45-minute lecture.

- If you choose to do a longer lecture, try using a "lecture-discussion" approach where the learners are encouraged to ask questions and engage in dialogue throughout the presentation. This will involve the learners more actively and will "break up" the lecture.

- Focus your presentation on a few key points rather than trying to cover too much material. You want the learners to leave with the most important information, and not be overwhelmed by the volume of content.

- Supplement your presentation with visual aids such as slides or handouts. Learning is more effectively reinforced through a multisensory approach (for example, hearing *and* vision). I suggest providing copies of handouts before the class so students can pay more attention to what you are saying rather than taking extensive notes as you are speaking.

Panel. A panel is a group of experts brought together to share their different perspectives on a topic. The advantages of panels over lectures are that they give learners several different points of view to consider, they provide learners with a chance to meet outside resources, and they offer a break from the traditional lecture approach. At the same time, panels require a lot of preparation ahead of time. Here are a few ideas to consider if you are thinking of using a panel:

- My experience is that students generally like getting the "outside" perspective that panel members can add to a topic. By inviting people who have different experiences, you can greatly broaden the learners' perspectives. For instance, in a workshop on working with cancer patients, a panel of cancer survivors can share their very different personal experiences in a powerful way that participants won't soon forget.

- Sometimes, if panelists bring different views to the table, you can give your students a chance to watch a debate on the topic. Here it is important to make sure that panelists are aware ahead of time that people with competing views will be on the panel so that they are not "blindsided." It is also important to make sure all panelists are treated with dignity and respect.

- Panels can be logistically problematic. Trying to schedule a group of presenters at the same time can be tricky. You also need to remember that you are asking people to volunteer their time and resources, and it's important to not take advantage of their good will.

- You will need to play a proactive role as moderator for the panel, making sure that all panelists are given time to present their ideas and guiding questions and exchanges in a way that balances free exchange, with respectful treatment of people who have given their time to be with your group.

Techniques for Teaching Skills

Here, the focus shifts to techniques that can be used in order to pass along new skills. These techniques are likely to be popular with adult learners because they involve drawing from the learners' experiences and giving them a chance to participate actively in the process.

These experiential learning techniques are essential in skills-based classes such as photography, dancing, learning an instrument, cooking, medical procedures, in-service for K–12 teachers on new discipline techniques, or learning a new computer application. While some presentation will usually be needed in order to introduce the skill, it is the opportunity to do activities during which you can *try out* what you are learning that make these techniques especially rewarding for learners. The two techniques for teaching skills presented here are demonstration and simulation:

Demonstration. A demonstration is basically a "show and tell" activity, where you teach something by first doing it yourself and then giving the participants a chance to try it out. This is an excellent technique to use when trying to help learners develop a new skill that builds on what they already know. It can also be used to teach something new and unfamiliar, although the instructor must remember that the participants are likely to learn something brand new at very different rates. In order for a demonstration to work, the instructor needs to be very well-prepared and to have worked out details and arranged for needed materials well in advance.

In my Facilitating Adult Learning class, the examples students have used to teach demonstration have been among the most interesting and creative techniques in the class. One student used demonstration to teach origami to the class. Another student interested in horticulture brought potting soil, containers, and plants in order to teach us how to pot small plants that we could then take home. Here are a few things to consider when using demonstration:

- Demonstrations are likely to be popular among your learners because they involve participants in the activity. So it's a good idea to use this technique at a point in your session when you know that the learners are becoming distracted or bored. It's a great "pick-me-up" activity.

- The key to a good demonstration is *preparation*. You need to be thoroughly versed in the technique and must be sure that all equipment is working. Trying to teach learners how to insert a video clip into a slide presentation when you are not able to access the Internet is going to be a disaster. Get there ahead of time and make sure everything is working.

- Make sure that participants have the supplies and tools that they need to practice the skill. Again, good preparation is the key.

- Remember that some learners may have disabilities or limited mobility that can affect how or whether they can participate in the activity. Be sure that all participants have a way to participate in some way and that no learners are singled out or not included because of a disability.

- Most of the time, demonstrations should be fun, because they are hands-on activities. You can make the experience more enjoyable, even if what is being taught is serious business, by being nonthreatening and making sure that you treat the learners in a way that will build their confidence, even if they are having difficulty performing the activity. A dancing student who is having trouble learning the steps of the tango may still be having a lot of fun just being there and trying to learn, so be encouraging and supportive, regardless of *how well* the person is doing.

Simulation. If you have every played SimCity or Flight Simulator on the computer or used a Wii or X-Box, you have experienced simulation. The purpose of simulation is to create a lifelike situation so that the participant can learn something by experiencing something close to the real-life experience. Jerry Gilley, in a chapter in Galbraith's *Adult Learning Methods*, describes simulation as a "dramatic representation of reality." Simulation can be based in technology, such as computer programs that simulate situations or high-fidelity human simulations (HFHS) used in the health professions to teach how to perform procedures on patients. Pilots spend a considerable portion of their training on a simulator. Other types of simulation may or may not be technology-driven. In-basket exercises, where a person is given several tasks to complete similar to those in the work setting, are one such example. Law enforcement training can involve simulating a crime scene and asking learners to "work" the scene using their investigative skills.

The main value of simulation is that it can be used to give learners hands-on experience with practical problem solving. It involves the learner actively in the process and is designed to help students learn and improve their skills. Considerations when deciding whether to use a simulation include the following:

- Can a simulation closely replicate the skills you are trying to teach?
- Do you have the equipment to conduct the simulation, and are there enough "stations" so that all participants can practice the simulation in the allotted time?
- To use a simulation effectively, you must have a solid background of experience in both the technique being taught and in how to operate the computer program or equipment used.
- Because a simulation is close to a real-life experience, it is a safe and efficient way to give learners experience with equipment and procedures when an error in real life can be very costly—such as flying an aircraft or performing a medical procedure.
- Simulation can also be a valuable practical experience when teaching skills that do not have such potentially critical consequences, such as office procedures or certain on-the-job tasks or practicing a sport or musical instrument.

Teaching About Attitudes and Values

Sometimes, what you are teaching won't be based on specific content or technical skills, but rather on helping learners develop understanding through self-exploration, reflection, and sharing with others. When I was completing my master's degree in counseling, other than a course on theory, we spent very little time mastering content from the knowledge base of the field. Rather, we focused on developing helping skills based on personal reflection and interaction with other learners. Here, the emphasis was on understanding ourselves and the attitudes and values that impacted how we worked with others in a helping relationship.

As a teacher of adults, much of your role will be to help adults learn to better understand themselves. Often, there is not a clear measurable outcome like "recall five theories of learning" or "develop a PowerPoint presentation." Rather, in these instances, you are trying to help learners come to terms with their basic beliefs and, sometimes, to expand or even change these views in order to help them function more effectively. Examples might include developing skills to more effectively communicate and work with others and learning to understand and appreciate differences among people based on race, class, gender, sexual orientation, or even different positions on the issues that are being discussed in your class. Here, the emphasis is on helping learners look inward to better understand personal beliefs, attitudes, and values (sometimes referred to as the "affective domain") in order to relate to others more effectively.

Many techniques can be used to explore the affective domain. For our purposes here, I will briefly cover discussion and role playing.

Discussion. Next to lecture, discussion is probably the most familiar technique for most teachers. There is no single "type" of discussion. Rather, discussion is often built into the class in conjunction with other techniques, including lecture. But discussion is perhaps the most important technique in working with adult learners because it gives them an opportunity to participate, to be heard, and to connect their own experiences to the topic.

For me, the most rewarding discussions happen when class members respond to one another's comments rather than just to mine. As learners interact with one another, and I am able to drift into the background for a few minutes, this is when really important learning takes place, because the group members are learning from one another. The following are some things to take into consideration in order to get the most out of discussion:

- Try to stay focused on the topic at hand. It's easy to drift off into side discussions and move away from the main topic. Staying focused is sometimes a challenge and, to be honest, I struggle with this because I often see connections between these side topics and the main focus of the discussion and, thus, sometimes allow discussions to stray a bit.

- Encourage wide participation from the group. Don't let one or two people dominate the discussion. Some instructors like to "call on" people to contribute. I personally like to leave it up to individuals to volunteer, because I know that some people may not be as comfortable speaking in front of a group. This is a matter of personal style, and you will have to decide how you wish to handle it.

- A key to good discussion is the ability to ask good questions. "Do you believe … " questions usually lead to limited discussion because there can be a yes or no answer. On the other hand, questions that begin, "What do you believe about … " or "If you were in this situation, what might you do?" are likely to stimulate more thoughtful responses. Asking "why" questions can also help facilitate discussion.

- Try to use both small- and large-group discussions. In small groups, people who are reluctant to share in front of the entire class may be more comfortable participating. In small groups, it is easier for more people to have a chance to share.

- A commonly used strategy is to break into small groups, ask the group to appoint a person to take notes (a "recorder"), and then reconvene in the large group. Then ask each recorder, in turn, to share one point from his or her group's discussion. Repeat this until all major points have been shared. You can ask groups to give their notes to you and later type them and share them as a handout with the entire group.

- If you plan to use a large number of small-group discussion activities during your class, consider setting up your room with individual chairs and tables, as discussed in Chapter Nine.

Role Playing. In role playing, a small number of participants act out a scenario based on the topic being discussed while the rest of the group observes and later provides commentary. Once the activity ends, the facilitator helps the group "process" the role play by asking questions about the experience and the issues brought to light by the scenario.

Role playing is a valuable technique for getting ideas out in a quick and relatively safe manner. However, my experience is that many learners are resistant to role playing, because they have to "perform" in front of a group. On the other hand, role playing is "safe" because the person is acting out the assigned role and not having to assume a personal position on the issue. Here are some tips for creating successful role plays:

- Always ask for *volunteers* to participate in a role play. Never select people from the group without their approval.

- Make sure the participants are clear about the roles they are playing in the scenario. Typically, a short written description of each role should be shared with the participant.

- A good role play is brief, five minutes at the most. The purpose is to create material for discussion through a scenario. If the role play is allowed to drag out, key points can easily be overshadowed by trivia and observers can become bored and distracted.

- It is essential that you take time to "process" the role play with the group. Ask the observers what they saw during the scenario. Ask the participants what it felt like for them to be in their roles. When dealing with an especially controversial or heated topic, make sure everyone has had a chance to debrief and that all are reminded that the role players were merely playing roles, not necessarily presenting personal positions.

Conclusion

This chapter is especially important for new teachers because it is about actually *doing* teaching. There is so much more that could be said about teaching techniques. But once you have developed some of the skills presented in this chapter, I encourage you to further explore the many creative ways that you can reach your learners. Once you do this, your repertoire of teaching tools will expand rapidly and you will be able to adapt your teaching to almost any topic or situation.

THINK ABOUT IT

Reflect on your experience as a teacher, especially over the past year or two. Make a list of some of the techniques you have used with your students. Which ones have seemed to work well? Which ones have not worked out so well? Why did the techniques you used work or not work?

Taking into consideration the degree of learner involvement, the purpose of the instruction, and your own background and strengths as a teacher, can you uncover patterns about your own teaching style? What are some of the things that you do best as a teacher? What are some things that you need to develop further?

Further Reading

Bowman, S.L. (2009). *Training from the back of the room*. San Francisco, CA: Pfeiffer.

Brookfield, S.D. (2013). *Powerful techniques for teaching adults*. San Francisco, CA: Jossey-Bass.

Brookfield, S.D., & Preskill, S. (1999). *Discussion as a way of teaching*. San Francisco, CA: Jossey-Bass.

Galbraith, M.W. (Ed.). (2004). *Adult learning methods* (3rd ed.). Malabar, FL: Krieger.

Silberman, M. (2006). *Active training* (3rd ed.). San Francisco, CA: Pfeiffer.

8

KNOWING YOURSELF

Understanding the Teacher Within

We have seen how knowing the content, knowing the learner, and knowing about teaching are keys to effective teaching. Yet one key, perhaps the most essential one, is still missing. This essential key is you . . . who you are, what you believe, and how you use your heart, mind, and abilities to reach the learners.

Two authors have written important books that highlight the "heart" of teaching. Earlier, I mentioned *Teaching from the Heart* by Jerry Apps. In this book, Apps discusses how looking inward is essential to becoming a teacher who can truly make a difference. Here's what Apps has to say:

> "Teaching from the heart comes from the depths of the teacher as a person. It is not only what the teacher knows, but *who the person is* [italics in original] that makes a difference. Teaching from the heart is an authentic endeavor. The teacher constantly asks, Is what I am doing truly an expression of who I am? And if it is not, why is it not?" (pp. 16–17).

He goes on to say that teachers make connections by striving to "touch the hearts of learners" and "encouraging people to take responsibility for their own learning."

Parker Palmer, author of the highly influential book *The Courage to Teach*, presents a similar view. He says, "good teaching requires that we understand the inner sources of both" our intentions and actions. Palmer asks readers to consider the question "Who is the self that teaches?" This book is built on the single premise that "*good teaching cannot be reduced to technique; good teaching comes from the identity and integrity of the teacher.*" Palmer states that his ability to connect with students has less to do with the "methods I use than on the degree to which I know and trust my selfhood."

Apps and Palmer make a convincing case for the need to look inward as an essential quality of the effective teacher. It's a view that I have shared for many years and, in fact, reading Apps and, later, Palmer led me to a transformation in my own approach to teaching. It made me more aware of the need to *share myself* with my learners. Good teaching is not just about helping learners master an area of content; it's also about helping them to grow as human beings, to find ways to integrate what they are learning into their own selves. Often this process is similar to what Jack Mezirow describes as "transformative learning."

Transformative learning involves a process of critical reflection, often resulting from a life-disruptive, or disorienting, dilemma. In transformative learning, a person goes through a process that ultimately leads to a new and different way of looking at the situation or at life in general. In the context of teaching and learning, it is important to remember that achieving transformation requires the learner to look inward . . . and this means the teacher must be able to do so as well.

Self-Understanding: The Heart of Effective Teaching

Many years ago, I completed a master's degree in guidance and counseling. As I mentioned in the previous chapter, the focus of this program was less on specific content mastery than on the process of developing skills, many of which are discussed in this book (for example, empathy, authenticity, respect) necessary to be a successful counselor. Although I have never practiced as a therapist, the experience of that program laid a foundation for what I have come to believe is essential to effective teaching. It's about the attitudes and values that we bring to our relationships with the learners. And this can only happen if we are willing to look inward and continuously question the assumptions we make and the values we hold about teaching and learning.

I believe there are four elements essential to knowing oneself as a teacher. These can be described as follows (another acronym . . . sorry!):

- History
- Reflection
- Technique
- Style

These letters, HRTS, can be pronounced "hearts," and they are the heart (yes, once again, the pun is intended) of this chapter. Let's turn now to each of these areas.

History

We are all influenced by our pasts. Who we are today is the product of our entire set of life experiences and, for this reason, no two of us are exactly the same. While the focus of this book is on current and future practice as teachers of adults, we can't overlook the importance of our own experience and the unique combination of personal history and personal characteristics we bring to our learners. In fact, many of our strengths, as well as areas in which we need to improve, have grown out of our vast life experiences.

Let me use my own story as a brief example. My father died after a long illness when I was six years old, and my grandmother died less than six years later. There is no question that these losses had a profound influence on the course of my life; yet at the same time, largely because of these losses, I believe that

I developed a sense of resilience—the ability to bounce back from adversity—that has served me well at difficult times over the years. I grew up in a working-class community and most of my family and the families of my friends did not have a college background. My mom always encouraged me to follow my dreams and to plan on attending college someday. So, although I was an underachiever in high school, I was still fortunate to be able to attend my hometown school, The University of Toledo. After struggling as an average student for the first two years, I made a deliberate commitment to work harder and did well in my final two years, as well as in my subsequent graduate work at Toledo and Syracuse. The point is that I was able to find a way to pursue my dreams and bounce back from adversity, even though the direction I pursued was not the norm or the expectation for most people in my community.

Think about your own history. What have been some of the forces that have influenced who you are? How have you handled success? How have you dealt with adversity? What are some of the forces in your life that have brought you to this point where you are teaching adults? Who are some of the people who played key roles in helping to shape your history?

Let me add one caution. While our histories are clearly a part of who we are, and it is important to understand and appreciate this history, it is also important to not become *trapped* by our histories. Unfortunately, for all kinds of reasons, many people are not able to look past the struggles in their past and move beyond their life circumstances. It is important to remember that our lives, our histories, are an evolving process; they are not locked in concrete. We *can* change and, indeed, much of what you do as a teacher of adults is to help learners realize that they can change, in ways small and large. But to do this, you will sometimes need to be able to revisit and even reinvent how you view parts of your own history.

Reflection

Earlier, we discussed the importance of experience in adult learning. It is especially important to remember that it is not merely *having* experience that matters; rather, it is how we are able to *reflect upon* and *make meaning* of these experiences that leads to the most important kinds of learning. This is the essence of transformative learning, mentioned earlier in the chapter. One of the most important aspects of knowing yourself as a teacher of adults is the ability to reflect on your practice and to use this reflection in order to better understand and question why you do what you do.

Donald Schön was an educator who was influential in introducing the notion of *reflective practice* to various professions, including education. According to Schön, reflective practice involves questioning one's assumptions or beliefs about practice and considering alternate possibilities when the original assumptions do not hold up or are, in fact, incorrect. Schön makes an important distinction between two types of reflection. One kind of reflection is what takes place "after the fact." You teach a class and, after it is over, you take time to reflect on the experience and, where needed, make adjustments for the next time. This is what Schön calls *reflection-on-action*. The other type of reflection is what takes place on the spot as a situation arises. For example, a piece of equipment does not operate or a guest speaker does not show up, or a confrontational exchange suddenly takes place between two students. You have to act on the spot to resolve the problem. If you have learned the skills of critical reflection, which in this case Schön would describe as *reflection-in-action*, you should—with experience—be able to resolve the problem, make a seamless adjustment, and move forward with the class.

Just as with your personal history, reflection means not being trapped by your past. It means that you reject the mindset of "I've always done it that way." To use the popular cliché, it means "thinking outside the box." Being reflective does not mean you automatically reject tried-and-true ways of doing things that have worked well over the years; rather, it means stopping to question the reasons for doing what you do and, when you realize that the old ways are not working like they used to, then you are open to exploring new strategies.

Technique and Style

The last two elements of knowing yourself, technique and style, go hand in hand and, therefore, I am going to discuss them together. *Technique*, as I am using it here, is the sum total of your knowledge and skills about how to actually perform the role of teacher. It has to do with your skill as a lecturer or discussion leader, how you prepare materials for your students, how you manage class time, and your ability to incorporate technology into your classroom. In other words, technique is all of the things we discussed in Chapters Six and Seven, about knowing the teaching-learning process.

In order to be an effective teacher, it is a given that you will have a certain degree of technical skill or technique. If you lacked even basic teaching skills, you would not be able to teach.

To give a couple of analogies, think of a violinist in an orchestra, or a painter, or a professional hockey player. These individuals have developed special skills that make them stand out. The skills were developed over many years of practice, learning, and more practice. It involved (at different times) trial and error, joy, frustration, fear, doubt, and elation. But we can safely assume that to get to the point where they are recognized as successful at their art or craft, they have been able to master a certain level of technique.

The same holds true for you, as a teacher of adults. You have entered teaching with some degree of experience, even if this is only limited to years as a learner who has witnessed first-hand plenty of very good and very bad teaching. As you start teaching and are able to reflect on your experience, you should continuously develop skills and therefore establish a technique for teaching.

However, technique alone is not sufficient. This is where *style* enters into the picture. Style is what allows each of us to stand out in our own way. In other words, style is what makes you . . . you! Style is what makes two people with similar technical skills perform in very different ways. Janis Joplin had a very distinctive voice. When I hear one of her songs, even one I have not heard before, I know instantly that she is the singer. For me the same holds true with classic rock artists such as Jimi Hendrix and Eric Clapton, or jazz performers like Miles Davis, John Coltrane, and McCoy Tyner. Each of these performers had (or has) a unique style that makes him or her instantly recognizable. To be sure, each demonstrates outstanding technical skill; but it is the unique, individual style that has allowed each to stand out and make a lasting contribution.

The same can be said for writers, artists, scientists, and people from virtually all walks of life. One can be very talented in what one does, but it is what is *unique* or *different* about what we do that separates us from the rest of the pack. Yo-Yo Ma is one of the world's greatest cellists. However, there are many, many cellists who have the ability to play many of the pieces that Ma performs in concert. What separates him from cellists in countless orchestras around the world is his unique style. There is something about how he performs, and it is that "something" that makes him stand out; this is what style is about!

Now, back to teaching adults. Does this mean that you are expected to be the Yo-Yo Ma or Jimi Hendrix of teaching? Of course not. What it *does* mean, however, is that you need to understand your own style and be able to play to that style. If your presentation skills are excellent and you are a dynamic speaker, you will want to take advantage of these skills. If you are very good at asking questions and helping learners to engage in dialogue, this should be an essential component of your style. If you are not a particularly dynamic lecturer, but have an ability to relate to your students as individuals, this will be a part of your style.

When I was an undergraduate, I had two "favorite" professors. One, the anthropologist I mentioned earlier, was dynamic, knowledgeable, and opinionated. He had a shock of red hair and a red beard, and regularly wore bib overalls to class (this was the early 1970s). Because he held strong opinions and had a forceful personality, he could sometimes be a bit intimidating. Yet, as I got to know him, I realized that he cared deeply for his students and was genuinely interested in them. The other professor was a psychologist. It was his class that I was teaching in the opening scenario of Chapter One. He was a kind, humble gentleman who smoked a pipe and regularly dressed in a suit and tie. His lectures were typically delivered in a very low-keyed manner. But he had valuable information, took a sincere interest in his students, and was readily available to meet to discuss class topics. These two men had styles that were like night and day, but I admired them both dearly, and each had an early and lasting influence on my desire to become a professor. The glue that connected these two teachers, and every other teacher who has made a difference in my life, is that they *cared* about the learners—about me as a learner.

A Closing Thought About Style and Caring

The final lesson I can share with you about knowing yourself is one you probably already know. Being an effective teacher of adults means many things, and it plays out in very different ways for each of us. However, as I said, the glue that binds all effective teachers is the quality of *caring*. A teacher can be strict, demanding, kind, awkward, challenging, unconventional, or traditional, but if she practices the skills I have shared in this book, she will be able to reach adults effectively. It matters less about what your actual style *is* than whether it is an authentic reflection of who you *are*. However, a teacher who does not care about the learners, or is unable to demonstrate this quality of caring, will be doomed to being, at best, a mediocre teacher. By demonstrating caring, you have upped the ante and immediately put yourself in a special place as a teacher of adults.

More than three decades ago, I ended my doctoral dissertation with a quote from Robert Blakely, a journalist who also worked in adult education, mainly in the 1950s and 1960s. I had the chance to see him give a keynote address at the 1980 Pennsylvania Association for Adult and Continuing Education Conference, where he closed with a quote that I believe still holds true today. He said,

> " … in our field the most important … the essential … quality is caring. The secret of all successful enterprises in helping adults to learn . . . is sympathy for, indeed, empathy with those who need and want to learn. It must be an informed sympathy flowing from deep and sensitive understanding. It must be an authentic concern based on a realization and valuing of a common humanity. It must be demonstrated in those ways that inspire in the learners a conviction of authenticity and understanding."

This quote spoke to me many years ago and still rings true today. The most important ingredient in effective teaching is **you**, and it is through qualities such as caring, empathy, and authenticity that you, as a teacher, can truly make a difference in the lives of the learners you serve.

Conclusion

As I have said, the ideas in this chapter are absolutely critical for anyone striving to be an effective teacher. You can master your content area, know something about the learners, and understand how to plan and implement instruction, but if you have not looked inside of yourself to understand who you are and why teaching matters to you, then you are missing a vital key. This reflective understanding completes the picture of you as an effective teacher.

THINK ABOUT IT

Write a statement of your personal philosophy of teaching adults. Don't worry about what others may think; this is just for you. Thinking about the elements of HRTS, plus the other three keys to effective teaching, write a statement that at a minimum considers the following questions:

1. *What do you believe about human nature?* Are people basically good or evil, or is human nature determined by one's environment?

2. *What do you believe about adult learners?* Do they have unlimited potential? Are they involved in learning because they are deficient in some area? Are they serious learners or are they just trying to get by with the minimum that is necessary?

3. *How do you view yourself as a teacher?* Are you a facilitator of learning, a content authority, a little bit of both? Do you think of yourself as caring, empathic, demanding, precise, reflective, decisive, flexible, or some other characteristics?

4. *How do the basic values you hold translate into how you teach, and why?*

5. *Have your ideas about teaching changed over the years or since reading this book?* In what ways?

Remember that this is a tentative statement, based on where you are *at this point in time*. Put this statement aside for now and pull it out every so often to look at it. See how you have changed and how you have remained consistent over time. Finally, I encourage you to revise, update, or even rewrite this statement from time to time to reflect major changes you may experience.

Further Reading

Apps, J.W. (1996). *Teaching from the heart*. Malabar, FL: Krieger.

Cranton, P. (Ed). (2006). *Authenticity in teaching*. New Directions for Adult and Continuing Education No. 111. San Francisco, CA: Jossey-Bass.

Mindlin, G., Durousseau, D., & Cardillo, J. (2012). *Your playlist can change your life*. Naperville, IL: Sourcebooks.

Palmer, P.J. (2007). *The courage to teach* (10th ann. ed.). San Francisco, CA: Jossey-Bass.

Pratt, D.D., & Associates. (1998). *Five perspectives on teaching in adult and higher education.* Malabar, FL: Krieger.

Schön, D. (1984). *The reflective practitioner.* New York: Basic Books.

Schwartz, B. (2005). *The paradox of choice.* New York: Harper Perennial.

Part Three

UNLOCKING DOORS TO EFFECTIVE TEACHING

9

CREATING A POSITIVE LEARNING ENVIRONMENT

Effective teachers pay close attention to the learning environ-ment. By learning environment, I mean those psychological, physical, and social factors that can influence learning. These can include such aspects as arrangement of seating, how the teacher handles the initial contact with learners, lighting, interaction among learners, class size, and the fair and equitable treatment of all learners.

In this chapter, we will begin with a look at climate setting and the psychological learning environment. Then we will shift to exploring the physical and social environments. We will also look at issues related to differences in the environment of large and small classes. Finally, we will briefly consider the role of tech-nology on the learning environment.

Climate Setting: Making a Difference from the First Meeting

I recall a class years ago when the instructor walked in and the first words out of his mouth were: "Most students are average, and the average grade is 'C'." You can imagine that caused a certain amount of discomfort among class members. Indeed, I'm pretty sure that several people dropped the class after that first meeting.

Contrast this approach with an instructor who greets students as they come into the room for the first class. This instructor welcomes the class and lets them know they are appreciated. Which approach would you prefer? Me, too.

The kind of climate you set from the very beginning is going to determine the tone of your class. Remember that many adults, especially those in adult basic education classes or those returning to higher education after many years, are likely to be nervous and even frightened. It has taken these learners a great deal of courage just to walk through the door. What you do in those first few minutes is going to set the stage for the entire course.

But climate setting is not only important in the first few minutes; it involves the psychological environment or tone of the class and matters from the first few moments of the class until the very end. What are some elements of a positive psychological environment? Here, I would refer back to the seven qualities of an effective instructor that were presented in Chapter Two. As a quick refresher, these are:

1. Building a climate of *trust*;
2. Showing an *empathic* understanding of the learners and their circumstances;
3. Being *authentic* or genuine in how you relate to the learners;
4. Demonstrating and modeling *confidence* in the learners and in yourself;
5. Balancing confidence with a degree of *humility* or modesty;
6. Showing *enthusiasm* for your topic, for the learners, and for simply being there for the learners; and
7. Demonstrating *respect* for the learners and for what you are teaching.

If you can work at developing these seven qualities, using some of the strategies outlined throughout this book, you will go a long way toward developing a psychological climate that is conducive to learner success.

The Physical Learning Environment

Think back on the last time you took a class. I want you to focus specifically on the physical classroom. How were the seats arranged? Was the lighting sufficient? How were the acoustics? Was the room too warm? Too cold? Did outside noise interfere with what was going on in the classroom? Was there enough room so that students were not too crowded? Was there *too much* room, so that you felt disconnected with others? Was the room free of trash and clutter? Did the technology work? Did the room have a comfortable or welcoming feel to it?

In many situations, the physical environment will depend on where the class is being held. Businesses and government agencies will often have "state of the art" facilities because they have the financial resources to invest in training. Several years ago, I held a class session at the training center of our local Air National Guard base. The facilities were excellent and I have to confess that I was quite envious. I have also attended programs located in businesses where the environment was highly conducive to learning. On the other hand, colleges and universities have facilities that often vary considerably in quality. Often, these classrooms have not been updated in some time. Public school adult education facilities and social service agencies often fare even worse.

So often, however, we overlook or just accept the physical classroom setting. Of course, as a teacher, you have to accept the hand you have been dealt. At my university, we can request certain rooms, but others may want the same room, so there is no guarantee that we will receive the room we prefer.

Now, I believe that effective teaching and successful learning can take place in almost any setting. The physical environment should not stop good teaching and learning from taking place. But I also believe there are things we can do to make the environment more conducive to learning. Here are some of the factors that can influence physical environment.

Lighting, Temperature, Acoustics, and Seats

Let's start with the bad news first. Here is where you might have to just accept the way things are. Try to provide as much lighting as possible. Remember that age-related changes in the eye make it necessary for older learners to have increasing levels of light.

Room temperature is a no-win situation. Regardless of the actual temperature, some learners will say its too warm, others too cold. My best advice (and its not all that great) is to just encourage learners to dress for comfort. Encouraging learners to layer clothing is usually more effective than trying to get the temperature of a large room adjusted.

Acoustics are also out of the teacher's control. But you should be aware of how your voice carries and adjust your speaking volume and tone according to acoustics, room size, outside noises, and, sometimes, the age of the learners. As with vision, there are normal changes in hearing that come with age. If you are teaching a group of older adults, remember that normal hearing loss may make it necessary for you to speak a little louder or in lower tones (since it is typically in higher tones where age-related hearing loss is common).

One tip here, though. Don't assume that vision and hearing issues are only related to age. Also, don't assume that I am only talking about the students; remember that, sometimes, you may be the one who is experiencing hearing loss. Effective teaching means taking care of yourself when it comes to factors that can affect your teaching. For example, I have for many years had a genetic hearing loss that is the opposite of age-related loss; I have difficulty hearing lower tones and have trouble hearing when there is lots of background noise. I have had this problem for a long time, but did not pay much attention to it until it really hit home a few years ago when I found myself having noticeable difficulty hearing some of my students in class. I realized that I needed to do something. The problem has improved since I began wearing hearing aids a few years ago, but I still sometimes ask students to repeat themselves when there are multiple conversations going on in the room.

As with room temperature, seats will probably never be "just right." Regardless of the style, some students are going to be uncomfortable in their seats. They can be too hard, too soft, too high, too low, and so forth. This is a legitimate concern, but there may be little you can do to change it. Typically, I take plenty of stretch breaks, and I tell students to feel free to stand up and move about the room at any time, including when I am presenting. After all, these are adults and they will know what they need to do to be comfortable. I find that it's best to be up-front and encourage them to feel free to do this; otherwise, they might be intimidated or feel as if they are being disrespectful.

Room Arrangement

Although you may sometimes be teaching in a room with seats that cannot be moved, most of the time, you will have the freedom to set up the seats (and tables if you have them) in different configurations. Of course, there are many ways to do this. Probably the five most common approaches are (1) seats facing the instructor at the front of the room, (2) the U-shaped classroom, with learners sitting in a U and the instructor at the front; (3) a rectangle or square; (4) a circle; and (5) seating in small groups at tables throughout the room. Each of these approaches has advantages and disadvantages and will work best under certain circumstances. Table 9.1 illustrates these seating arrangements and some considerations when using each approach.

Other Considerations

A number of other factors can influence the physical learning environment. Some of these are described below.

Standing, Sitting, or Moving? It may seem trivial at first, but the decision about whether you should sit, stand, or even walk

Table 9.1 Five Types of Seating Arrangements

Arrangement	Considerations	
Traditional	Works best in large classes Emphasizes the instructor Works well when using media presentations (for example, video or slides) Discourages interaction among students	
U-Shape	Learners face each other; encourages interaction Instructor at front, can see and interact easily with all participants Students may have trouble seeing people on the same side of the table	
Rectangle or Square	Similar to U-shape, but places instructor in less conspicuous location Sometimes hard to see people on the same side Works especially well in small seminar or boardroom setups	
Circular	Especially good in setups with chairs but no tables Instructor does not stand out, but is part of the circle Stresses equality among participants Works best with small or medium groups	
Individual Tables and Chairs	Ideal when doing lots of small group work Can be used with round or square tables Some participants may have their backs to the instructor By focusing only on those at one's own table, interaction with class members at other tables may be reduced	

around the room while teaching has important implications for climate and physical environment. Let's take a closer look.

Standing. Traditionally, the perception is that the teacher stands in front of the learners. This puts the teacher in a position of authority and leadership. In a large class, standing makes it easier to see all students, and for them to see you. It also gives a certain *presence* that conveys an image of expertise and confidence.

Sitting. While standing is the most common approach, especially in large classes, when teaching a smaller class of about four to twelve students, it can feel awkward, intimidating, and even foolish to stand in front of and over the group. In this situation, sitting levels the playing field and can create a more informal climate. I find that sitting works best when the group is relatively small and I have a clear sight line to all learners (such as in a U-shaped, rectangular, or circular room arrangements). The disadvantage of sitting is that the instructor can sometimes lose presence in the group. This isn't usually a problem in a small classroom; it is more of a problem when making a conference presentation, especially before a large group.

Moving around the room. In many room arrangements, moving about the room while teaching will bring you closer to the learners. When you are moving among tables or standing in the center of the room, you are "coming to" the learners. Most of the time this will work well; but on occasion, there is a chance that students could perceive this as "spying" on them and what they are doing while you are talking. I realize that sometimes students are texting, sending emails, or reading something on the Internet unrelated to the topic, but I prefer not to police the classroom. You may decide that a different approach works best for you.

Amenities. Sometimes, the learning environment can be enhanced by small amenities. In my early years, with small classes, I used to bake and bring banana or orange bread to my classes on certain evenings. Now I often bring candy to class or I will bring small items such as a mini-slinky to give as a *stress-reducer* or *conversation starter*. For years, I have taught many of my classes in a weekend format (Friday evenings and all-day Saturday); in these classes, I invite the learners to take turns bringing snacks on Saturday morning. I would not suggest to you that candy, snacks, or toys are a game changer ... but I do think they can help lighten things up a bit and bring the group together, especially when class sessions are long.

The Social Environment

The psychological climate and physical environment of a class are important considerations in effective teaching. But there is still another dimension that can impact the setting—the social dimension of the learning environment. In a nutshell, the social environment is about recognizing and valuing the ways in which our learners, and we ourselves, are different. We often use the word *diversity* to describe these differences. Here, I am referring to differences based on gender, race, class, sexual orientation, disability, and age, along with other factors where there is potential for discrimination, be it intentional or, more often, unintentional.

An important aspect of effective teaching is how one creates a welcoming climate where *all* learners are valued and have a voice, not because they are different, but because of how these differences can enrich the learning environment. While some differences, such as gender, race, and some physical disabilities, are usually visible and easily recognized, others such as class, sexual orientation, or learning disabilities, may not be obvious, unless a person identifies as such. I suggest that you not make assumptions about the backgrounds of your learners. For example, don't assume that none of your students are lesbian, gay, bisexual, or transgendered (LGBT) just because they do not *say so*. Again, don't assume anything, but be sensitive and aware in such ways as using inclusive language like "spouse or partner," instead of just spouse, or not automatically assuming that one's spouse is of the opposite sex.

For the most part, in this discussion I am assuming that there are differences between intentional and unintentional discriminatory behaviors. When a learner or teacher deliberately makes racist, sexist, or homophobic comments, this problem will have to be confronted directly and immediately. But quite often, discriminatory comments or practices are subtle and sometimes unintended. As an example, some teachers may tend to call on male students more frequently than female students (and there is research evidence to support that this happens). Is it deliberate or is it just a habit of which one is not even aware? It really doesn't matter; what matters is that the teacher become aware of the problem and change the behavior.

Here are a few thoughts that you might want to consider in order to create a learning environment that values *all* learners.

1. *Assume that your students have a diverse range of backgrounds and experiences.* If you start with this assumption, you can work from the outset to create an environment that is welcoming of and sensitive to all learners.

2. *Don't avoid discussing differences just because it may feel uncomfortable.* For example if you are teaching a course where race and racism are a part of the content, don't avoid the topic for fear of offending the students of color in your class. If the topic is pertinent, overlooking it out of possible discomfort is selling yourself and your learners short and can even be perceived as disrespectful.

3. *Treat all students in an equitable way.* It's a subtle difference, but I prefer to emphasize *equitable* rather than *equal* treatment. Treating people "equally" fails to take into considerations the differences that learners bring to the class; equitable, on the other hand, means that everyone is treated

in a fair and just manner, while taking into consideration their past experiences and individuality.

4. *Don't single out students because of their gender or race and expect them to represent "the view" of women or minorities.* It is both disrespectful and unfair to ask an African American student, "So, Denise, what is the Black perspective on this question?" Don't assume that Denise, or any other student, can be expected to speak for all people of the same race.

5. *Be sensitive to the needs of students with disabilities without singling them out.* If I know a student has a disability, I will ask him or her in private what I can do to accommodate his or her needs (of course, the Americans with Disabilities Act offers legal guidelines here, but I believe that sometimes just asking the person is a more genuine way to help). If you have not worked with students with disabilities in the past, it might be helpful to look at a few resources to gain some basic tips. For example, when working with deaf students via an interpreter, you should speak directly to the student, not the interpreter. This may seem like common sense, but many teachers fail to do this simply because they are unaware.

In summary, the social environment means creating a *safe space* for learning, where all learners are valued and treated in an equitable manner. It is where you, as a teacher, play an important role in setting the tone by modeling the kind of practices that will ensure an environment of trust and openness.

Large vs. Small Classes

Two additional aspects of the learning environment are important to consider. These are differences in teaching approaches based on class size and the influence of technology in the classroom. Let's look at class size first.

Clearly, there are going to be differences in how you work with small, medium, and large sized classes. Some things you can do with a class of fifteen are just not feasible with a class of 100 students. In larger classes, it obviously becomes more difficult to get to know most of the students and to individualize learning activities. At the same time, those who have a more dynamic teaching style are likely to thrive in this setting. In smaller classes, it is easier to get to know the learners better and to give them more freedom to take on activities of personal interest.

However, there are certain commonalities regardless of class size. These are the seven attributes of an effective teacher that I discussed in Chapter Two. It does not matter whether you are teaching five students or 500, you will be a more effective teacher by creating an environment of trust, showing empathy for the learners (especially when they come to you with individual concerns), being yourself (authenticity), showing both confidence and a degree of humility, being enthusiastic, and demonstrating respect for the learners. While you may have to adjust how you demonstrate these qualities based on class size, the qualities themselves are essential. Also, the four keys to effective teaching from Chapter Two—know the content, know the adult learner, know about teaching, and know yourself—matter regardless of class size.

Teaching in a Connected World

No doubt, the most obvious change in the world of teaching over my more than three decades as an educator has to do with technology. Not to date myself, but when I was a graduate student, I wrote first drafts of my papers and dissertation longhand, which was traumatic given my terrible handwriting (just ask my students) and I used punch cards and the mainframe computer on campus to do my data analysis. When I first began teaching, technology consisted of handwritten overhead transparencies that would yellow and smear quickly, plus reel-to-reel or VHS films and audiocassettes. I bought my first computer (a Kaypro II) in 1984 during my second year as a professor.

Today's technology is obviously a game-changer in the world of teaching, and an instructor who does not make use of technology runs the risk of being seen as obsolete. This does not mean that you need to be a technology expert or that you need to use some form of technology in every class activity. Rather, it means that you need to know enough to know what technologies can help you better reach your students and under what circumstances. For example, if you are going to present lecture material, you will almost certainly want to supplement your comments with a visual tool, such as PowerPoint or Prezi. Again, you don't need to know the whole range of available tools. But you do need to keep up enough to know what will best work for you and your learners.

Since technology is changing constantly and because there are excellent online and print resources as well as training opportunities to help keep you up-to-date, I am not going to go into specific information about technology in the classroom. However, I do want to offer a few tips that have helped me over the years to get more out of technology in the classroom.

1. Because of technology, you can communicate with your learners at any time from anywhere. If you come across an article or a video resource that you think would benefit students, you can share it right then and there. The trick here is to avoid overloading students and keeping your communication limited to the most important information.

2. Use technologies that will best help you reach your students, but be careful to avoid overkill. Do you really want to spend twenty hours developing a video for a five-minute segment of your class when a few PowerPoint slides or a handout will work just as well?

3. Always try out your technology before you unleash it on your class. So often, teachers (including me) come up with

a technology-based presentation, only to find when they get to class they are not able to use it.

4. Have a backup plan. Inevitably, whether you are a novice or expert with technology, you will have glitches. If you have a backup (such as a second computer or tablet, or if you send a handout electronically to class members before class), you can make a fairly seamless transition from one mode to another.

5. Finally, don't be afraid to ask for help. Of course, technology is a place where being self-directed becomes important. But this involves knowing when to ask someone else for ideas and advice. In the classroom, remember that many of your students may know more about technology than you do; if you get stuck with something, don't be afraid to ask one of the students for help.

I don't want to be trite and end the section by saying something simple like "technology is your friend." But in today's world, it *is* a part of effective teaching. If you can recognize this and find ways to incorporate aspects of technology into your teaching, I am sure it will be worth your time and effort.

Conclusion

The kind of environment you create in your classroom will go a long way toward determining the quality of the learning experience. Although you may not always have control of all environmental factors, especially the physical classroom setting, the tone that you create in terms of climate setting and social environment will play a large role in how students respond to your teaching. Although you will have to make adjustments based on class size, the same basic principles hold true. Finally, in today's world, technology plays a crucial role in teaching adults and will inevitably be a part of any learning environment.

THINK ABOUT IT

Using a class that you have recently taught, conduct an "environmental audit," where you reflect on the psychological, physical, and social learning environments to determine which aspects of that environment may have enhanced or detracted from learning. Make a list of the factors discussed in this chapter and then write down some notes about these elements.

Can you identify some factors that may have hindered learning? Which of these are factors over which you had no control? What might you have changed to facilitate more successful learning? How might you use this information about learning environments to make changes, now and in the future.

Further Reading

Hiemstra, R. (Ed.). (1991). *Creating environments for effective adult learning.* New Directions for Adult and Continuing Education No. 50. San Francisco, CA: Jossey-Bass.

10

OVERCOMING RESISTANCE TO LEARNING

As teachers, we want to believe that we have the best interests of the learners at heart and that our learners truly want to be involved in the activity. But we know realistically that this is not always the case. The purpose of this chapter is to introduce the concept of *resistance to learning* and to explore some strategies for recognizing and dealing with this problem.

Resistance to Learning

Imagine yourself in a windstorm. You are walking into the wind to reach your destination. You have to push yourself against the force of the wind gusts. You tire quickly and your muscles become tense. It takes most of your strength to move forward. Now imagine the same walk without the pressure of the wind. Much easier, right? Basically, this is what resistance is about. It has to do with what pushes against us or keeps us from moving forward.

Knud Illeris, an educator from Denmark, writes about situations when learning does not occur. He describes three kinds of situations. The first of these is *mislearning*, where a person simply learns something incorrectly. We've all had times when, for whatever reason, we just don't "get it." The problem here is that once we mislearn something, its very hard to *unlearn*. A second situation is what Illeris calls *defense*. This is when learners may reject ideas outright. It can occur in situations where long-held beliefs are being challenged or when someone just does not want to learn a new way to do something. Defense is kind of like a shield that "protects" a person from letting ideas get through. The third situation Illeris describes is *resistance*.

Illeris points out that resistance can be either negative *or* positive. Negative resistance is what typically comes to mind; these are forces, like the wind in the above example, that restrict or restrain forward movement. However, he also says that there are times when resistance can be positive. In today's world, where we are bombarded with information—the Internet, social media, twenty-four-hour news cycles, and the like—we have to make choices about what we pay attention to and what we *choose* to ignore. This is what Barry Schwartz refers to as "the paradox of choice," in his book by the same name. We simply have to make choices in order to manage our lives in today's world.

Let me share an example. Gardening is one of the activities I most dislike. I have resisted doing yard work my entire life and, at this point, I see no reason to change. Oh, I enjoy looking at flowers as much as the next person; I just prefer not to learn about how to become a successful gardener. I would rather spend my time doing other things (like writing this book). To summarize, then, according to Illeris, learning resistance can have a positive side, because we have to make choices about where we are going to put our time and energy and what we are willing to trade off in order to do so.

In a nutshell, resistance involves forces that restrain or restrict movement toward change. Here are a few words that describe resistance:

Fight   Repellence
Opposition   Rebuff
Defiance   Refusal
Repulsion   Blocking
Withstanding

Resistance can be general or situational. Some individuals are just resistant by nature. We all know people who are generally disagreeable and who hold out against any sort of change. But most often, resistance is situational. A person may simply not be in the mood to learn under a certain set of circumstances. When conditions change, the resistance may fade.

Reasons for Resistance

Adults may be resistant to learning for many reasons. Let me share several examples:

1. *Previous negative experiences.* Many adults come to you with a history of negative past experiences. For example, adults who participate in literacy or high school equivalency programs bring memories of failure, fear, and frustration from their early schooling experiences. People who dropped out of college when they were younger and are now returning years later as adults also are likely to have had negative experiences. As a teacher, a big responsibility will be to help the learners have a very different experience that will allow them to overcome their pasts.

2. *Mandatory participation.* While we know that most adult learners choose to participate voluntarily, there are times when they are required to attend training, workshops, in-service programs, or other educational activities. Sometimes people just have a tendency to dig in their heels when being told what to do. One of my former students, Dr. Jonathan Taylor, developed a scale to measure resistance to mandatory training. The scale showed promise in his research on resistance among police officers in a mandatory training program.

3. *Perceived irrelevance.* One of the most frequent problems that can lead to learner resistance is the belief that what one is learning is of little value and will not make a difference. Here your understanding of the topic is important, because you can focus on the areas you know are most relevant to what you are teaching. It is also where an understanding of motivation strategies can be used to make the topic relevant.

4. *Situational factors.* Sometimes, resistance can be caused by factors that have nothing to do with the topic, content, or teacher. Adult learners can't always leave their problems at the doorstep when they come to your class. Sometimes, learners bring family problems, work issues, or health concerns to the learning activity. If you are not feeling well or are worried about something else going on in your life, chances are you will be distracted. This distraction can sometimes be strong enough that you may resent having to participate in the learning activity and, thus, are resistant.

5. *Choosing not to learn.* Learning is a choice that each of us makes, and sometimes, we may simply choose *not* to learn about something. There are people who just don't *like* to engage in learning activities. They would rather spend their time doing other things. If you are teaching in an informal setting, where people have chosen to participate, this is not going to be a serious problem. But in cases where learners find themselves required to participate, those who don't wish to be involved may show resentment, hostility, or anger at having to be there.

What Can You Do?

What can you do to help break down learner resistance? To be sure, there are times when you won't be able to reach some learners and you will need to find a way to just get through the session without having these people disrupt your efforts to teach. But most of the time, there are strategies that you can use to help overcome resistance. Stephen Brookfield, in *The Skillful Teacher*, has identified several strategies for overcoming resistance. Let me share a few of these:

1. *Ask whether the resistance is justified.* Do the learners have a reason for being resistant? Have they been required to attend? Is your session being held at a time when the learners are busy

with other responsibilities? An accountant who is required to attend a workshop in the middle of tax season is likely to be under stress and, thus, frustrated at having to take time away from the job to attend a learning activity. In a case like this, I would argue that the resistance is justified and the solution is simple: schedule the program at a different time of the year.

2. *Sort out the causes of the resistance.* As we have seen, there are many possible reasons for resistance. If you are finding many of the learners are resisting, it will be helpful to find out the reasons. If there is one main reason, such as resentment over being required to attend, then you can focus on that one factor. On the other hand, if you find that there are many different causes for the resistance, then it will probably take some time to work with the learners to sort out the causes and try to come up with solutions. Of course, when you only have a short time, like one or two hours, with the learners, this is not very practical. You may need to try some of the other strategies instead.

3. *Involve students in planning.* One of the central tenets of good adult education practice is to involve the learners in the planning process. I strongly encourage this and try to practice it myself when possible. However, research on whether involving learners makes a difference has shown mixed results. Basically, it has been found that, while learner satisfaction increases with learner involvement, there does not appear to be a significant increase in achievement. In other words, involving the learners in the planning process is likely to lead to greater satisfaction, but not greater achievement. When breaking down learner resistance, it might just be the case that involving the learners will help win them over and reduce the resistance.

4. *Explain your intentions clearly.* It seems like common sense to tell learners up-front what you plan to cover in your session.

However, many trainers or facilitators forget to do it. One way to break down resistance is to give the learners a clear "heads up" about what you are going to do and why you are doing it. This is consistent with what Knowles says in his first assumption of andragogy, which was discussed in Chapter Five.

5. *Involve former resisters.* Brookfield says that one of the best ways to break down resistance is to enlist the help of people who previously were resisters. Former resisters know the problems that may lead to resistance, and sometimes they can convince others to let themselves become engaged in the learning activity.

6. *Work to build trust.* This strategy works best when you are with the learners over a period of time, rather than in a brief training session. As you will recall, trust is one of my "seven words" for teacher. We discussed trust earlier, but it's worth restating here that, in cases when resistance is caused by a lack of trust (in the teacher, in the topic, in the organization), there is much you can do to create a climate in which learners are willing to "let their guard down" and engage in the activity.

7. *Strike a bargain with total resisters.* Finally, there are times when, no matter what you do, a learner is simply not going to work with you. In such cases, you need to ask whether it is worth spending an unreasonable amount of time trying to win someone over who is "unwinnable" or whether you should focus on those who are interested in learning. My experience is that in a group of twenty-five learners, I would rather spend my time and energy on the twenty-three who want to be there, or at least are willing to try, and to leave the other two alone, as long as they do not disrupt the session or distract the other learners. You can't always reach everyone, and its ok to not feel responsible for those few learners who

are just not interested. While this may sound like admitting failure, I prefer to look at it as serving the greatest good for the majority of learners.

There is one more thing to remember about resistance to adult learning. We have a popular phrase in the adult education world: "Adults vote with their feet." If an adult learner is not happy or satisfied with a learning experience, he usually has the freedom to leave. And, indeed, there are times when adult learners will do just that. They will overcome their resistance by opting out. Of course, such is not the case in mandatory situations. Most of the time, this is not what you want to have happen. This is where strategies such as those above can be particularly useful.

A Personal Experience

As I have said, resistance is something that happens to each of us at one time or another. To bring this chapter to a close, I would like to share an experience of a time when I was the resister. Many years ago, our department held a daylong retreat where we had a guest facilitator focusing on team-building activities. The retreat was held at the end of spring semester, just after we had submitted final grades. It had been a difficult year both for the department and for me personally. While I normally would be open to a team-building workshop like this one, I knew that I just did not want to be there at that particular time. While I did not speak out, my body language clearly conveyed displeasure and resistance.

At lunch more than one of my colleagues pulled me aside and asked what was wrong. When I simply said, "I just don't want to be here today," I felt kind of foolish. We went back to the afternoon session and I did my best to contribute to the session. In hindsight, this was clearly not one of my proudest moments as a learner, but it taught me that, like anyone else, I could be caught up in the resistance mode under the right circumstances. Thus, the experience provided me with a valuable learning experience and some insight into how one can become a resister under certain circumstances.

Conclusion

Resistance is often overlooked, but it can be a very real issue if not addressed in an open, honest way as soon as it arises. The ideas I have shared in this chapter are a good start. But perhaps, in the long run, the most useful tool for overcoming resistance is an understanding of *motivation* and how it can be used to enhance the learning experience. We will look at motivation in the next chapter.

THINK ABOUT IT

A. Think of a time when you found yourself resisting a learning experience. It can be a formal class or a training activity in the workplace. What was the cause of the resistance? How did you feel when you were experiencing the resistance? Were you able to resolve the situation? Did the instructor try to intervene in some way? Take a few minutes and write a paragraph or two about the experience, like I did with my experience above.

B. Think of a time when *you* were the teacher and had to deal with a resistant learner. Do you remember how you felt? What strategies did you use to try to engage the learner? How well did these work? Using some of the ideas presented in this chapter, would you try any of them if this situation arises in the future?

Further Reading

Brookfield, S.D. (2006). *The skillful teacher* (2nd ed.). San Francisco, CA: Jossey-Bass.

Taylor, J.E. (2010). *Resistance to learning in mandatory training contexts: Design and construction of a diagnostic instrument.* Unpublished doctoral dissertation, University of Tennessee.

11

MOTIVATION

When teaching adults, few topics are more important to understand than motivation. But motivation is also very elusive. There is much confusion and uncertainty about what motivation is and what it is not. This is largely because we cannot *see* motivation; we can only infer it. In addition, the term itself is often misused. Motivation is *not* a verb; it is not something that one person *does* to another. Thus, you cannot "motivate" your learners any more than a football coach can "motivate" his players. However, you CAN create conditions that can enhance a learner's motivation.

In this chapter, I will share some ideas to help you better understand this elusive concept. By the end of the chapter, you will be able to describe two key elements of motivation and you will have learned a number of practical strategies you can use to increase the likelihood that your learners will, in fact, be motivated to learn.

What Is Motivation?

According to the APA *Dictionary of Psychology*, published by the American Psychological Association, motivation is "the impetus that gives purpose or direction to . . . behavior and operates at a conscious or unconscious level" and it is "a person's willingness to exert physical or mental effort in pursuit of a goal or outcome." In other words, motivation has to do with how much a person desires to make the effort to pursue a certain goal.

The word that lies at the heart of motivation is *need*. Basically, a need is a gap, or discrepancy, between what "is" and what is "desired." Thus, the greater the gap between what is and what is desired, the greater the motivation will be. Think of a basic drive like hunger. A person who is very hungry, that is, who has a strong need for food, will be more highly motivated to seek food than someone who has just had something to eat.

In the world of learning, the need is a gap between what the learners know and what they "need" to know. Let's say that I need to know how to use Skype in order to communicate face-to-face with my students between class sessions. If I have never used Skype, then the gap will be wide and the motivation should be high. On the other hand, if I already know the basics of Skype but just need to learn one or two new features of the program, then my need may not be as strong.

Howard McClusky, who was a pioneering figure in the adult education field from the 1940s through the 1980s, proposed the "Power-Load Margin" formula as another way to explain need in relation to motivation to learn. McClusky made the following distinction:

> Power = a person's supply of resources. These include energy, time, money, desire, family support, and so forth. Power is finite and varies from person to person, and varies within a person from time to time as life circumstances change.
>
> Load = a person's responsibilities. These include work duties, family obligations, health level, lack of time and money, and so forth. Load is the sum of a person's obligations and current life circumstances.

The Power-Load Margin formula holds that the likelihood one will be motivated to participate in learning is the person's level of Power minus current Load. Thus, a person who is energetic, wishes to learn, has the time available, and the money to pay for a class will be much more ready to learn than a person who has recently developed a chronic health condition and has had to assume more responsibilities at work.

Two Important Concepts in Motivation

It is important to remember that there is no single theory of motivation. Rather, there are many theories based on different ways of thinking about motivation. While a detailed discussion of motivation theories is beyond the scope of our discussion in this book, I do want to introduce two concepts that, together, are essential to understanding motivation to learn. This is the notion of Expectancy-Value Theory. Simply stated, this view holds that

$$\text{Motivation} = \text{Expectancy} \times \text{Value}$$

where

Expectancy = the belief that I can be successful in learning something

and

Value = how important it is to me to learn it

Let's look at a couple of examples. Say that Sarah wants to learn to play the piano. She studied the clarinet in high school and so she has some familiarity with music and is confident that she can apply this knowledge toward learning a different instrument. At the same time, it is important for her to learn to play the piano because she wants to set an example for her young daughter, who will be taking lessons in another year. In Sarah's case, the belief that she can be successful in learning the piano is high (expectancy) and it is important to her to invest in doing so (value). Thus, we could expect that Sarah's motivation to learn to play the piano is high.

On the other hand, Bob has been invited by a group of friends to join a sailing club. The problem is that he does not know how to sail and finds that the skills needed to be a good sailor are very difficult to learn. In addition, he has never been very interested in spending time on the water. Thus, even though Bob would enjoy the camaraderie of being a part of the group of friends, he is not very confident that he can learn the needed skills (expectancy) and, since he has never particularly enjoyed water sports, his interest level is low (value). It would follow, then, that Bob's motivation to learn to sail would be low.

The problem with understanding Expectancy-Value Theory is that most situations are not as clear-cut as the above examples. It's not all or nothing. Levels of expectancy and value range on a continuum from low to high. Sometimes a person may value what she is learning but may lack the confidence to be successful. At other times, the person is confident about learning something, but does not see the value in doing so. And at still other times, the person may have moderate levels of expectancy and value; here it would be expected that motivation level would be somewhere in a middle range.

It is especially important to remember that, when working with adult learners, your job is twofold: (1) to show adults that they can, in fact, learn successfully and (2) to show that what you are teaching is worth learning. In the next section, I will share some practical strategies that you can use to enhance motivation among your adult learners.

Strategies for Increasing Learner Motivation: The ARCS Model

In 1980, when I was a graduate student at Syracuse University, I took a course on motivation and instruction, which was taught by John Keller, now a retired professor at Florida State University. Throughout this course, we studied many different theories of motivation. Some theories focused on the expectancy dimension, while others emphasized the value aspect. But what I found especially useful was a model of motivation that Keller developed and called the ARCS model. Originally developed for use in the K–12 classroom setting, the model has been adapted to many settings over the years, including training and adult learning. According to Keller, instructors can increase learner motivation by paying attention to four things:

- Attention
- Relevance
- Confidence
- Satisfaction

This means that, in order to be a motivating instructor, you must use strategies that will (1) get the learner's attention; (2) demonstrate that what you are teaching is relevant to the learner; (3) build confidence that the students can, in fact, learn what is being taught; and (4) demonstrate that there is a "payoff" for the learner. Keller offers many different strategies for achieving each of the ARCS model elements. I would like to share a few examples to show that you can use these very practical approaches quickly and easily to reach your own learners.

Attention

You already know that getting and keeping learners' attention is essential to successful learning. How can you do this? One strategy is to arouse curiosity *using controversy or conflict*. Or you can share a surprising piece of information (Did you know that … ?). Sometimes, saying something provocative will get attention quickly and will start a discussion.

You can also gain attention by doing something that is out of character for you, which learners will notice right away and it will grab their attention. I have been known to walk into class wearing a Viking hat or a scary mask, especially around Halloween. Because this is out of character for me, it definitely gets attention quickly and gives the class a good laugh.

Another way to get attention is by using humor. Now this is a tricky one because it can come with risks. I'm a terrible joke-teller. I can't remember most jokes and, when I can, my timing with the punch line is usually off. Yet I am able to use humor in many other ways. Humorous examples and stories can work very well. Most of the time, I turn the humor on myself. I want to stress that, when using humor, you need to be careful not to single out learners and "use" them to make your point.

Still another way to grab learners' attention is to involve them right away. Using an activity or asking a question that can lead to discussion turns the focus on the learners, and they are likely to respond by paying attention and contributing to the activity.

But getting the learners' attention is just a start. The real key is to know how to *hold* their attention once you have it. Keller's other three strategies will help you do this.

Relevance

What can you do to show learners that what they are learning is important or worthwhile? Perhaps the most useful strategy for doing this is to draw from the learners' experience. We have discussed the importance of learner experience throughout the book, and here it is again. If you can connect what you are teaching to the life experiences of the learners, they should immediately see the value of the topic. If you are doing safety training with people who apply pesticides, you can begin by asking for examples of when participants have been in potentially dangerous situations. Your topic is immediately relevant to anyone in the group who has ever experienced a similar problem.

Another way to let learners see that the topic is relevant to them is to let them know what they will be able to "take away" and use immediately. A guitar instructor who says, "I want to show you three chords, and if you can learn them, you will be able to play dozens of new songs," has given learners something to take with them and use right away. At the same time, it's also important to show that what you are teaching will have value in the long term. *"Taking the time to learn this basic information now will make it a lot easier for you when you get to the next level."*

Still another strategy to make the learning relevant is to give learners the chance to make choices whenever possible. While you may need or want to make key decisions about what you are going to teach and how you will do it, if there are places where you can offer options, it can make it easier for the learners to see the value of what you are teaching.

Confidence

To increase the learners' expectations that they can succeed, your job is to find ways to help build confidence. First, be clear about what is expected. In my graduate classes, I routinely prepare a syllabus that includes all course requirements. Students know what to expect and they know that I'm not going to surprise them with a "pop quiz" or extra writing activity later in the term. If you tell the learners what you are going to do and what you will expect them to be able to do, there will be few surprises. When a teacher does this, the learners have a chance to take in what is expected of them and realize that they can, in fact, do it. Of course, the more you can reinforce that they have the ability to meet the requirements, the more confidence they are likely to develop.

Another aspect of confidence building is the question of difficulty. How difficult should you make your course or program? My experience suggests that there is an "optimal" level of difficulty: difficult enough to be challenging and motivating, but not so difficult that most people cannot succeed. I often tell my students that my role is to push them toward the edge of the cliff, but not to let them fall over.

We have all heard of teachers who take pride in making their classes so difficult that a large number of students do not pass or receive a high grade. Is this a difficult instructor or a poor one? I think that when most students do not do well, much of the problem lies with the instructor not knowing what an appropriate level of difficulty is.

Still another strategy for building learner confidence is to provide opportunities for learners to be successful. Keller states that these success opportunities should be different for someone who is just beginning to learn about the topic than for someone with more experience who is striving for "mastery." For example, if you make the first assignment one you know all or almost all of the students will be successful at, you will have taken a step early on to build learner confidence.

Finally, as with the other motivation strategies, it is important to consider the learners' experience. The more the learner is able to exercise control—such as engaging in problem-solving activities or projects that involve making choices—the greater the opportunities for building confidence.

Satisfaction

The final element of the ARCS model is satisfaction. What is the *payoff* to the learner or, as Keller asks, "What is satisfying to you as a learner?" For the college student, this can be passing a course with a good grade. A music student might find satisfaction in being able to play a new piece of music. A third grade teacher may find satisfaction in being able to use the new whiteboard in her classroom. An adult in a Bible study class may feel satisfied that he now has a better understanding of the New Testament. This final element of the ARCS model has to do with sustaining motivation *after* the learning experience is over.

Of course, one of the greatest rewards is being able to use what one has learned. If the learning activity was relevant (value to the learner) and if strategies were used to build confidence (expectancy for success), then evidence of satisfaction should be there.

There is an important distinction between intrinsic and extrinsic motivation. *Intrinsic* motivation is when rewards come from within the learner (such as a sense of achievement, confidence in being able to apply what was learned, curiosity about learning more about the topic, and satisfaction with what has been learned), whereas *extrinsic* motivation is when rewards come from outside of the person (such as grades, praise, or incentives such as pay raises or promotions). There is much research on the relative value of intrinsic and extrinsic motivation, and the results are often controversial. I encourage you to see the value in *both* intrinsic and extrinsic rewards, but to try to understand the motives of your learners. If a group of workers is participating in your training program because they will receive a raise, then extrinsic motivation strategies will probably be most effective. On the other hand, if the motive is to learn a new skill for personal growth, such as painting or ballroom dancing, then the motivation will be intrinsic and the rewards will come from within. As the facilitator, the better you are able to understand this distinction and how it fits with the motives of your learners, the more likely you will be to use motivational strategies that lead to learner satisfaction.

Another Approach: Five Pillars of a Motivating Instructor

Raymond Wlodkowski is an educator who, like Keller, has written extensively about motivation. As a final perspective on understanding motivation, I would like to share the five characteristics Wlodkowski identified as "pillars" of a motivating instructor:

- Expertise
- Empathy
- Enthusiasm
- Clarity
- Cultural Responsiveness

According to Wlodkowski, *expertise* means knowing the content and knowing how to teach it to others. *Empathy* means understanding the learners and demonstrating caring for them. *Enthusiasm* means that we value what we are teaching, we are committed to what we do as teachers, and we are able to convey this to our learners. *Clarity* means making sure that learners are able to understand what we are teaching, and *Cultural Responsiveness* means creating a safe learning environment that is respectful of all learners.

You will notice a bit of overlap between these pillars and the seven attributes and "Elements of Effective Teaching" that I presented in Chapter Two. I actually include empathy and expertise as two of my seven words for a teacher. Expertise and Clarity are similar to the elements, Know the Content and Know the Teaching-Learning Process that I present in Chapter Two. Wlodkowski's cultural responsiveness is somewhat similar to how I use the word respect. This overlap of concepts is understandable because these are ideas that have been created, developed, and refined by educators, philosophers, psychologists, and others over the decades. They transcend any single theory or approach to learning and teaching.

Conclusion

In closing, I want to restate that motivation is a very complex, misunderstood topic. Yet, it is crucial when striving to teach adults effectively and there are steps you can take to increase or enhance the motivation of your learners. If you can put the ideas offered in this chapter into practice, you should be able to address many of the concerns associated with low motivation in learning.

THINK ABOUT IT

Think about a class or workshop that you are scheduled to teach in the near future (or one that you taught recently). Using the four areas of the ARCS model, come up with at least two strategies that you could use to increase learner motivation. Write these down and use them when you teach the session.

- Which strategies did you use?
- How well did the strategies work?
- How did you feel when you were using the strategies?
- Which of these strategies would you like to use in the future?
- Are there other strategies that you might have used?

    If possible, share these with a colleague and ask the person to share her own experiences in dealing with motivation issues experienced in her own teaching.

Further Reading

Keller, J.M. (1983). Motivational design of instruction. In C.M. Reigeluth (Ed.), *Instructional-design theories and models: An overview of their current status* (pp. 383–429). Mahwah, NJ: Lawrence Erlbaum Associates.

McClusky, H.W. (1970). An approach to a differential psychology of the adult potential. In S.M. Grabowski (Ed.), *Adult learning and instruction* (pp. 80–95). Syracuse, NY: ERIC Clearinghouse on Adult Education. (ERIC Document Reproduction Service No. ED 045867.)

Pink, D.H. (2011). *Drive: The surprising truth about what motivates us.* New York: Penguin.

Wlodkowski, R.J. (2008). *Enhancing adult motivation to learn* (3rd ed.). San Francisco, CA: Jossey-Bass.

12

DEALING WITH DILEMMAS AND CHALLENGES

In the previous chapters, I have shared an approach to teaching adults built on seven essential teacher attributes and four keys to effective teaching. If you adapt these ideas into your own teaching, I am confident you will be well on your way to being an effective teacher of adults. However, we know that things happen, and the road is not always a smooth one. All teachers face problems, difficulties, and even ethical dilemmas along the way. While it is not possible to know exactly what these will be or when they will pop up, having an idea of what you might expect can help you to be ready to "reflect-in-action" as mentioned earlier, so that you can minimize difficulties before they become serious problems.

The focus of this chapter is on several kinds of challenges you may face when teaching adults. Some of these have to do with your own fears and doubts, while others deal with conflict among students, and still others are ethical questions that you may need to address at some point. Again, I don't suggest you automatically assume you will face these problems, but it is important to not be taken by surprise if they *do* happen.

Facing Your Fears About Teaching

You are getting ready to go to your first class, and you're scared. This is normal! In fact, if you weren't at least a little apprehensive, you really *would* have something to be worried about! Again, having fears is normal and, fortunately, there are things you can do to minimize these fears. I would like to discuss three different kinds of fears: "pre-game jitters," the imposter syndrome, and over- and under-preparing.

Pre-Game Jitters

You've no doubt heard about athletes, musicians, actors, or other performers who have the jitters before they perform. It's a way to get ready or to get "psyched" to perform. This same principle holds true for the teacher who engages in the professional artistry of teaching. Sometimes, though, pre-game jitters are taken to an extreme. Glenn Hall, a Hockey Hall of Fame goaltender, was rumored to have vomited before every game in order to overcome his jitters. I hope your own jitters come nowhere near this extreme. But they are real nonetheless.

In my early years of teaching, I would pace back and forth in my office, clutching my notes and trying to do a last-minute review. I can even feel the jitters in my stomach as I write this and remember those early years. Over time, the discomfort became less intense, but has never left altogether. In fact, if I don't feel some *anticipatory jitters* before a class, I am uncomfortable because it means I'm really not ready to go.

How can you deal with pre-class nervousness? First, remember that this is normal. Its actually a way of your body and mind telling you to build up your energy and concentration so that you can release it at the right moment. There is no single strategy for calming nerves that works for every person. I try to shut my office door fifteen or twenty minutes before class and enjoy a few minutes of solitude.

One strategy that has worked for me over the years is to listen to music. In a recent book entitled *Your Playlist Can Change Your Life*, Galina Mindlin, Don Durousseau, and Joseph Cardillo show how you can create playlists for your MP3 player to help you deal with different situations in life. I recently took their advice and created a short playlist that I call "Gear Up." I often play it before I go to class. I try to include songs that will make me feel good and start my juices flowing. While the songs change from time to time, my current Gear Up playlist consists of "Wonderin'" by Neil Young, "JuJu Man" by Dave Edmonds, "Restless Wind" by String Cheese Incident, "Why Baby Why/Tiffany Queen" by McGuinn, Clark, and Hillman, and "Mama Don't" by J.J. Cale. I can tap my toes, drum on my desk, and sing along (quietly!). These are fun songs that energize me and loosen me up so I'm ready to go.

Imposter Syndrome

A second type of fear is what psychologists Pauline Clance and Suzanne Imes called the "Imposter Phenomenon." This is when a person, in spite of what she knows or has achieved, feels like a fraud who does not deserve acclaim for what she has accomplished. Stephen Brookfield, in *The Skillful Teacher*, writes about this with regard to teachers and teaching. It's a common problem and understandable when you realize that a group of learners has chosen to gather, often paid money to do so, to learn about something that you know. Humility probably contributes to your self-doubt, but here is another place where your confidence or *attitude* can balance out the doubts. Remember that you are there for a reason; because you have worked hard to develop expertise in your topic. Also, remember that the learners will bring their own experiences with them; you *don't* have to know it all. By drawing from the learners' experience and blending it with your expertise, you should be able to reduce the imposter syndrome.

Over-Preparing or Under-Preparing

A third fear that nearly all of us have at one time or another is: "What if I don't have enough material to fill the class time?" Relax. If you have thought through your topic and used a planning process like the one presented in Chapter Six, you will have thought through this problem ahead of time. But the reality is that most of us speak somewhat more quickly in a class or presentation setting than we do in normal conversation, so we may go through a presentation more quickly than planned.

A common solution for many teachers is to over-prepare and to try to cover much more material than is realistic to include. This creates a different set of problems. The teacher is likely to feel pressured to "get through" the material, even if it means not spending as much time on the really important areas. The focus shifts from making sure the most important material is covered to beating the clock by going through it all.

However, there is a middle ground where you add and delete material as needed in order to keep to a schedule. First, as suggested in Chapter Six, identify those concepts and ideas that are most important to cover. Then consider the difficulty of different topics so you can determine what percentage of time should be devoted to them. Third, rehearse your presentation before you teach it and reduce the time by 10 to 25 percent, depending on how quickly you normally speak.

Perhaps my best advice when deciding how much to prepare can be found in the idea of *lagniappe*. The term is mostly used in the Gulf Coast region of the United States, especially in and around New Orleans. It essentially means "something extra," such as a merchant giving a small gift to a customer or adding a thirteenth donut to a dozen. In the way I'm using it here, it means preparing an extra activity or topic, which can then be added if you run out of material or can easily be left off if you run out of time. I often keep an extra activity in my personal "toolbox," such as a video or a small group discussion activity that I can add if we finish too soon. To be honest, I usually don't need it, but it reduces my anxiety to know it's there . . . just in case.

Disruptive Learner Situations

One of the things I love about teaching adults is that I don't often have to deal with discipline problems. My wife taught middle and high school for forty years and we have many good friends who are K–12 teachers. I regularly tell them how much more difficult I believe their jobs are, mainly because they have to deal with many more discipline problems than I do.

But just the same, those of us who teach adults *do* sometimes face discipline problems or disruptions in class. This is especially true in situations where participants are required to attend, like mandatory training or ABE/GED programs that are required in order to continue receiving financial assistance from the government. While there are some tips for addressing these problems in Chapter Ten, "Overcoming Resistance to Learning," sometimes the problems go beyond those solutions. Here are a few examples of problems I have faced over the years and how I have addressed them.

> *Problem:* Side conversations between students that become loud and disrupt the rest of the class.
>
> *Resolution:* I often stop speaking and just look at the students until they notice me and stop talking. No need to say anything directly to them; they'll get the message with minimal awkwardness, except perhaps for a little embarrassment.
>
> *Problem:* Two students get into an argument about a particularly controversial or heated topic.
>
> *Resolution:* I play a diplomatic role as I model respect for both parties. If one party feels that he has been "attacked," I try to negotiate between the individuals to clarify the situation. Sometimes this works, but often it is necessary to discuss the problem further with the individuals. If this is necessary, I usually do it individually outside of class.
>
> *Problem:* A student tries to dominate the class by making excessive observations, non sequitur (irrelevant) remarks, or by intimidating other class members.
>
> *Resolution:* Sometimes this can be addressed simply by speaking with the student in private and trying to help

her understand that what she is doing is having a negative effect on the overall climate of the class. Sometimes
the learners will take the matter into their own hands and
"call" the person; in extreme cases, I have seen a group
"shun" a particularly disruptive group member. In very rare
cases, it may be necessary to take more serious action, such
as asking a person to leave the class or reporting the behavior to a higher authority. Overall, I recommend using the
least punitive measure, *unless* you have reason to believe
that there is a risk of physical harm to anyone.

Again, you will probably find that you do not have to face
many conflict situations. But be ready in case they arise. Your
responsibility as the instructor in such situations is twofold: (1)
to take steps to ensure that the trusting classroom environment
is not violated and (2) to deal swiftly with any situation in which
there is a risk of physical or psychological harm to anyone in
the class.

Cheating and Plagiarism

Another problem area has to do with cheating. If you are teaching
a class where no grades or evaluations are given, you can probably
skip over this section; but for those of us responsible for assigning
grades and other forms of evaluation (for me, this includes sign-
ing off on comprehensive examinations and dissertations), it is
necessary to be aware of the possibility of cheating.

Let me say from the outset that I believe most students do
not cheat and I do not spend a lot of time safeguarding my classes
against cheating. By overemphasizing cheating, I believe it potentially penalizes the vast majority of students who would not think
of doing so. But you still have to be on the lookout for cheating
and, if you find it, you need to have a way to deal with it.

Plagiarism is a very specific form of cheating. It is where one
takes the writing of another and claims it as one's own, without

giving credit to the original author. In today's world, with the widespread use of the Internet, search engines like Google, and social media like Facebook and Twitter, it can become easy to forget that plagiarism is a serious problem. Over the years, I have had to deal with plagiarism on several occasions, including course assignments, comprehensive exams, and even a dissertation proposal. In some cases, the student pleaded "ignorance," saying he did not realize that what he was doing was wrong. In most cases, though, the person admitted to using the work improperly.

Plagiarism is a serious problem in academic life. Many scholars, including well-known historians and best-selling authors, have damaged their reputations because they have used the words of others without giving appropriate credit. In today's world, where vast resources are only a few keystrokes away on Google, Wikipedia, and other search engines, the risk of plagiarism will likely continue to rise. Here are a few strategies I have found helpful to reduce the risk of plagiarism:

1. Avoid creating competitive classroom situations, like grading on a curve, where one student's grade is dependent on how others in the class perform. In some fields, such as business or the legal profession, the culture is often based on competitive "win-lose" situations. In such cases it may be necessary to create a competitive climate. But most situations, especially those involving non-credit, informal adult education classes, are not conducive to competition. So why encourage it in the first place?

2. Encourage students to share resources with one another when working on projects as long as they are clear that it is expected the final product will be their own work. This is another way to build trust in your class and to encourage students to draw from their experience to help one another. Again, however, it is important to stress that the final product must be original work.

3. Communicate clearly with students about plagiarism and what could be the consequences of plagiarizing an assignment. After two recent incidents of plagiarism in one of my classes, I have begun to include a statement about plagiarism in my course syllabus, so that students are informed up-front. I emphasize that if students have questions about what constitutes plagiarism, they should simply come and ask me for clarification!

4. Finally, remember that you have access to the same search tools as your students. When a writing style seems "choppy" or involves words or phrases that do not seem like they were written by a student, I have "googled" them and found that they were, in fact, lifted directly from some other source. While you don't want to have to spend a lot of time tracking down possible plagiarism, it might be helpful to let students know up-front that you have access to the same search engines as they do, and what they can find, you too can find.

As I have said, this is one of my least favorite parts of teaching, and it's probably the one thing in this book that I do not like having to write about. But it can be a real problem, and overlooking it is naïve. So I suggest that you put it on the table from the outset, and then don't dwell on plagiarism unless you actually suspect or find it.

Professional Distance

As a teacher, you will need to decide how formal or informal you wish your relationships with students to be. This will be a matter of personal preference and comfort level and ties directly to your own style as a teacher.

When I say professional distance, I'm referring to how close you get to your students, how much you share about yourself, whether you encourage or allow for contact with students outside the classroom, and how open you are to having students share their personal situations with you, particularly when it relates to completing course activities in a timely way.

The extent to which you prefer a formal or informal style will depend largely on your own style, preference, personality, and, sometimes the setting in which you are teaching. For example, most people who teach non-credit or informal classes or work in training situations probably find it easier to be informal. In higher education, the degree of formality varies from instructor to instructor. My best advice is to do what is most comfortable for you. But remember that if you are working with adult learners, they may be put off by an instructor who insists on formality, especially when you are of similar ages.

I am typically uncomfortable with formality and, thus, try to create an informal learning environment. When I began my teaching career, I was younger than most of my students. Thus, I encouraged my students to call me Ralph, and still do today. Probably half to two-thirds of them do so. I realize that some students, especially those who are younger or are from different cultures, are uncomfortable with this informality and prefer "Dr. Brockett" or "Dr. B.," and that's fine as well.

I often meet with students off campus, usually at a local bookstore or café, to work on their research proposals or dissertation chapters and sometimes for general advising. I give out my home phone number and tell students it is fine to call me within reason. I encourage students to share openly with me if they are having difficulties and, as a result, they sometimes share personal situations with me. In this sense, I view my role as a caring listener and resource, but do not believe it is appropriate for me to try to "solve" their concerns. Finally, I typically suggest that the last class be held at an off-campus restaurant where we can meet, wrap-up the class, and have some time to socialize informally.

Again, this is my own approach. I share it as one example, but am not saying this is the approach you should necessarily adopt. You should do whatever allows you to build trust, respect the learners, and demonstrate authenticity.

Let me add a quick comment about dating or intimate relationships with students. Regardless of whether you are responsible
for evaluating student learning (such as giving a grade) or not,
there is a *power differential* between you and the student. By virtue
of being the instructor, your role is different from that of the students. Therefore, there is always a risk that you could, even unin-
tentionally, put a student into an awkward, uncomfortable, or
exploitive situation by engaging in a dating relationship, regardless of who initiates the relationship. For this reason, I strongly
encourage you to avoid dating students, at least until the course
is over or until the teacher-learner relationship has ended.

Should You Share Your Own Views
with Learners?

Finally, an area that often poses an ethical dilemma for teachers of
adults, as well as educators in general, is the question of whether
it is your responsibility as a teacher (1) to present information in
a "neutral" way, avoiding sharing your own positions, especially
on controversial topics, (2) to advocate certain positions that are
important to you as an authority on the topic you are teaching, or
(3) to use your role as teacher as a "bully pulpit" to indoctrinate
students toward your way of thinking. A good resource for the
neutrality/advocacy/indoctrination issue is *Rights and Wrongs in
the College Classroom* by Jordy Rocheleau and Bruce W. Speck.

Like it or not, the classroom is a political space, and teaching
is a political activity. The key is to be clear about where your
politics lie, and how (or if) you wish to communicate your own
views, preferences, and biases to students.

This is where differences in teaching philosophies may be
of help. If you believe that your primary responsibility is to
present ideas to learners and to let them decide what positions
to take, then you may lean more toward neutrality. On the
other hand, if you believe that your role as an educator is to
actively let your views be known and to support those ideas

closest to your heart, then you may be more comfortable with an advocacy role. Of course, it is possible to take a middle position somewhere between these two extremes, and this is perhaps the most common response to the issue.

One way to approach the neutrality versus advocacy question is to look for a balance between authenticity, where you act in a way that is genuine or true to yourself, and respect, where you actively encourage and value the free exchange of ideas among students. If you can find a way to achieve both, then perhaps you have found a good balance for you.

But what about indoctrination? Basically, indoctrination is an extreme form of advocacy. The instructor will often take a self-righteous posture and use the position of power to cajole or overpower learners into adopting his or her position. Taken to the extreme, it can involve singling out and humiliating students who resist the instructor's dogmatic stance. Clearly, indoctrination impacts trust in a negative way, puts the instructor in a light that is overconfident and lacking in humility, and is disrespectful of the learners' views. Thus, it is a clear violation of many of the seven essential qualities of an effective teacher described in Chapter Two and, in fact, often crosses the boundary into being unethical.

Conclusion

Throughout this book, I have emphasized that teaching adults is most often a highly rewarding and satisfying activity. Adults bring great potential to learn and, when paired with the knowledge and skills you bring to the situation, there is much that you can do to help them reach their goals. At the same time, as in any human activity, there are certain issues or problems that need to be addressed. If you take the time to reflect on the kinds of dilemmas I have raised in this chapter and have a way to deal with them if, in fact, they do arise, then you should be able to put these concerns aside and focus on your real purpose . . . bringing out the best your learners have to offer!

THINK ABOUT IT

Pick one of the dilemmas from this chapter or one that you have experienced as a teacher and consider how you resolved the problem. Jot down a few notes to help you recall the incident.

Now, using what you have learned in the previous chapters, compare what you did at the time with what you would likely do now. What is different about your original response? Similar? To what extent do you believe that the approach you take to the problem can directly affect the outcome?

Further Reading

Brockett, R.G., & Hiemstra, R. (2004). *Toward ethical practice*. Malabar, FL: Krieger.

hooks, b. (1994). *Teaching to transgress: Education as the practice of freedom*. London and New York: Routledge.

Rocheleau, J., & Speck, B.W. (2007). *Rights and wrongs in the college classroom*. Bolton, MA: Anker.

EPILOGUE

Now You're Ready ... Go and Teach Adults

Actually, you have probably figured out by now that you actually had the basics for teaching adults before you read this book. I hope, though, that the book has provided some tools to help you along the way and even a framework to organize your thoughts as you prepare for your next opportunity to teach adults. In this Epilogue, I would like to briefly summarize the main ideas of the previous chapters and bring the book to closure with a couple of observations.

Seven Attributes

The seven qualities or attributes of an effective teacher that I presented in Chapter Two permeate the entire book. As you may have noticed, these qualities came up at different times in most chapters. Of course, a great many qualities can be found in effective teachers of adults, not just these seven. However, I didn't want to overwhelm you with a huge list, and keep in mind that these seven are easy to remember since they spell out "teacher."

Trust, empathy, authenticity, and respect are basic qualities essential for any helping professional. Counselors, nurses, physical therapists, as well as teachers, need to possess these crucial attributes. They are basic qualities that set the tone for the teacher-learner relationship.

Confidence and humility are the yin and yang of teaching. Both are essential, and the key is to find a balance between the two. Too much confidence is likely to result in arrogance and the perception of being on an ego trip. At the same time, too much humility can lead you to downplay your knowledge, skills, and credibility. A balance between confidence and humility should help you to come across as having authority and possessing expertise, while acknowledging to learners that you are still, in fact, a student of your topic and are continuing to learn new things. A true "expert" is someone who never stops learning and readily admits this to others.

Finally, enthusiasm is what holds the rest of the qualities together. Adult learners can sense your enthusiasm, or lack thereof, and will pick up on it. Enthusiasm is contagious. If you demonstrate this quality to your students, they are likely to become interested in what you have to say, even if they don't share your level of enthusiasm. But, as each of us probably can attest from our own experience, a teacher who lacks enthusiasm will have a very hard time getting us to care about the topic.

The Four Keys to Effective Teaching

The centerpiece of this book has been what I call the four keys to effective teaching. You probably already knew that each of these areas is important to good teaching, but by breaking them down as I have, I hope I've been able to give you a way to differentiate among the keys and to help organize your thoughts about the essential components of effective teaching. Knowing the four areas breaks down the teaching-learning process into manageable pieces. If you start by looking at these areas separately, you can keep from being overwhelmed by what you need to know about teaching adults effectively. Then, *later* you can pull them together into the package that is you … the teacher!

Two Credos

Each of us needs to have a way to regularly remind ourselves of what most matters to us as teachers. You might think of these as "catch phrases" or credos. They are short statements of what you believe, which you can repeat regularly until they are fully integrated into your mindset. I have two credos that I use to guide what matters most to me in teaching adults. I shared the first of these in an earlier chapter. It is that, for me, *bringing out the best in my learners is what I strive to achieve*. My other credo is something that came to me a few years ago: *I would rather spend my time and effort building people up than tearing them down*.

Now I realize that it is not possible to live by these beliefs in all situations. There are times when I am going to have to critique the work of students and, in order to act with integrity, there are times when I will have to be the bearer of bad news to students. But even so, my credos can guide me in how I handle such situations. Except in extreme cases such as deliberate plagiarism, I will try to help students learn from their mistakes in a way that gives them hope for improving in the future. Rarely do I shut the door on the possibility that someone can improve; thus, even when I have to play the role of the "heavy," I can still do so in a way that gives learners the hope that they might be able to reach their best in the future. It takes time to develop this ability, but with reflection and understanding, you can incorporate the skill into your own repertoire.

A Final Word

The final lesson I would like share with you about teaching adults is one that you probably already know. Being an effective teacher of adults means many things, and it plays out in very different ways for different teachers. However, the glue that binds all effective teachers is the quality of **caring**. Teachers can be strict, demanding, kind, awkward, unconventional, or traditional, but if they practice the skills I have shared in this book, they will be able to reach adults effectively. I said this earlier in the book, but it bears repeating: it matters less about what your actual style *is* than whether it is an authentic reflection of who you *are*. But a teacher who does not care about the learners or about what he or she is teaching, or is unable to demonstrate this quality of caring, will be doomed to being, at best, a mediocre teacher. By demonstrating caring, you have upped the ante and immediately put yourself in a special place as a teacher of adults. The quote in Chapter Eight from journalist and educator Robert Blakely reflects this perspective very well.

With that, I wish you a most rewarding journey as you go forward and teach adults.

References

Apps, J.W. (1996). *Teaching from the heart.* Malabar, FL: Krieger.

Bowman, S. (2008). *Training from the back of the room.* San Francisco, CA: Pfeiffer.

Brockett, R.G., & Hiemstra, R. (1991). *Self-direction in adult learning: Perspectives on theory, research, and practice.* London and New York: Routledge.

Brookfield, S.D. (2006). *The skillful teacher* (2nd ed.). San Francisco, CA: Jossey-Bass.

Brookfield, S.D. (2013). *Powerful techniques for teaching adults: A practical guide.* San Francisco, CA: Jossey-Bass.

Caffarella, R.S., & Daffron, S.R. (2013). *Planning programs for adult learners* (3rd ed.). San Francisco, CA: Jossey-Bass.

Cavaliere, L.A. (1992). The Wright brothers' odyssey: Their flight of learning (pp. 51–59). In L. A. Cavaliere & A. Sgroi (Eds.), *Learning for personal development.* New Directions for Adult and Continuing Education, No. 53. San Francisco, CA: Jossey-Bass.

Clance, P.R. (1985). *The imposter phenomenon.* Atlanta, GA: Peachtree Publishers.

Dean, G.J. (2002). *Designing instruction for adult learners* (2nd ed.). Malabar, FL: Krieger.

Galbraith, M.W. (Ed.). (2004). *Adult learning methods: A guide for effective instruction* (3rd ed.). Malabar, FL: Krieger.

Gilley, J.W. (2004). Demonstration and simulation. In M.W. Galbraith (Ed.), *Adult learning methods* (3rd ed.). Malabar, FL: Krieger.

Houle, C.O. (1988). *The inquiring mind* (3rd ed.). Norman, OK: Oklahoma Research Center for Continuing Higher and Professional Education. (Originally published in 1961.)

Hiemstra, R. (1994). Helping learners take responsibility for self-directed activities (pp. 81–87). In R. Hiemstra & R.G. Brockett (Eds.), *Overcoming resistance to self-directed learning.* New Directions for Adult and Continuing Education, No. 64. San Francisco, CA: Jossey Bass.

Hiemstra, R., & Sisco, B.R. (1991). *Individualizing instruction*. San Francisco, CA: Jossey-Bass.

Illeris, K. (2007). *How we learn*. London and New York: Routledge.

Keller, J.M. (1983). Motivational design of instruction. In C.M. Reigeluth (Ed.), *Instructional-design theories and models: An overview of their current status* (pp. 383–429). Mahwah, NJ: Lawrence Erlbaum Associates.

Keller, J.M. (1987). Strategies for stimulating the motivation to learn. *Performance & Instruction, 26*(8), 1–7.

Knowles, M.S. (1975). *Self-directed learning: A guide for teachers and learners*. New York: Association Press.

Knowles, M.S. (1980). *The modern practice of adult education* (rev. ed.). New York: Association Press. (Originally published in 1970.)

Knowles, M.S. (1989). *The making of an adult educator*. San Francisco, CA: Jossey-Bass.

Knowles, M.S., Holton, E.F., III, & Swanson, R.A. (2011). *The adult learner*. Oxford, UK, and New York: Taylor & Francis.

McClusky, H.W. (1970). An approach to a differential psychology of the adult potential. In S.M. Grabowski (Ed.), *Adult learning and instruction* (pp. 80–95). Syracuse, NY: ERIC Clearinghouse on Adult Education. (ERIC Document Reproduction Service No. ED 045867.)

Merriam, S.B., & Bierma, L.L. (2014). *Adult learning: Linking theory and practice*. San Francisco, CA: Jossey-Bass.

Merriam, S.B., Caffarella, R.S., & Baumgartner, L.M. (2007). *Learning in adulthood* (3rd ed.). San Francisco, CA: Jossey-Bass.

Mezirow, J., & Associates. (2000). *Learning as transformation*. San Francisco, CA: Jossey-Bass.

Mezirow, J., Taylor, E.W., & Associates. (2009). *Transformative learning in practice*. San Francisco, CA: Jossey-Bass.

Mindlin, G., Durousseau, D., & Cardillo, J. (2012). *Your playlist can change your life*. Naperville, IL: Sourcebooks.

O'Donnell, K. (2006). *Adult education participation in 2004–2005* (NCES 2006–77). Washington, DC: National Center for Education Statistics.

Palmer, P.J. (2007). *The courage to teach* (10th anniv. ed.). San Francisco, CA: Jossey-Bass.

Rocheleau, J., & Speck, B.W. (2007). *Rights and wrongs in the college classroom*. Bolton, MA: Anker Publishing.

Schön, D. (1984). *The reflective practitioner*. New York: Basic Books.

Schwartz, B. (2005). *The paradox of choice*. New York: Harper Perennial.

Silberman, M. (2006). *Active training* (3rd ed.). San Francisco, CA: Pfeiffer.

Taylor, J.E. (2010). *Resistance to learning in mandatory training contexts: Design and construction of a diagnostic instrument*. Unpublished doctoral dissertation, University of Tennessee, Knoxville.

Thorndike, E.L., Bregman, E.O., Tilton, J.W., & Woodyard, E. (1928). *Adult learning*. New York: Macmillan.

Tough, A. (1979). *The adult's learning projects* (2nd ed.). Austin, TX: Learning Concepts. (Originally published in 1971.)

Tyler, R.W. (2013). *Basic principles of curriculum and instruction* (1st ed., rev.). Chicago, IL: University of Chicago Press. (Originally published in 1949.)

VandenBos, G.R. (Ed.). (2007). *APA dictionary of psychology*. Washington, DC: American Psychological Association.

Wlodkowski, R.J. (2008). *Enhancing adult motivation to learn* (3rd ed.). San Francisco, CA: Jossey-Bass.

Index

Page references followed by *fig* indicate an illustrated figure; followed by *t* indicate a table; followed by *e* indicate an exhibit.

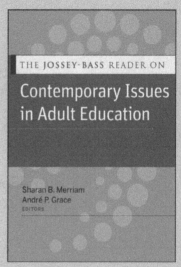

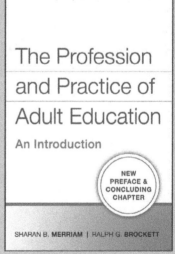

Want to connect?

Like us on Facebook
www.facebook.com/JBHigherEd

Subscribe to our newsletter
www.josseybass.com/go/higheredemail

Follow us on Twitter
http://twitter.com/JBHigherEd

Go to our Website
www.josseybass.com/highereducation